To my friend &
co-worker Garrett!
I hope my mom's experiences
inspire
you!
Lots of
appreciation
for your
support.
Lucia

Building Bridges of Understanding

Building Bridges of Understanding

My Personal Quest for Unity and Peace

By Lucía De García

- Library of Congress Cataloging in Publication (CIP Data)
De García, Lucía
Building Bridges of Understanding

I. Biographical 2. Inspirational I. Title

Cover Design by Luis Sánchez
(Lucía's Photo by Michael Landa)

2nd Edition

IBSN 0-9776373-0-I

Published by Élan International
620 Newport Center Drive, Eleventh Floor
Newport Beach, California U.S.A.
Tel: (949) 559-5507
WWW.ELANINTL-USA.COM

Also By Lucía De García
"My Pilgrimage to Holy Places, A Renewal of my Spiritual Life"
An Anthology of Stories to Inspire, Encourage, and Enjoy.

To order please contact:

Élan International
620 Newport Center Drive, Eleventh Floor
Newport Beach, California U.S.A.

Tel: (949) 559-5507
e-mail: Lucía.deGarcía@cox.net
WWW.ELANINTL-USA.COM

Printed in the United States of America by Printmedia Books
www.printmediabooks.com

The book *Building Bridges of Understanding* may be purchased at special discounts for non-profit, educational, and business organizations.

A portion of all proceeds of this book will be donated to The Jane Goodall Institute (JGI)

About the Author

Lucía De García is the Founder, President, and CEO of Élan International based in Newport Beach, California. Élan assists both foreign and domestic enterprises in Latin American business practices, opening new markets and expanding market share throughout the hemisphere. She is the Founder of the Multicultural Institute for Leadership (MIL), a Trustee of the Jane Goodall Institute (JGI), a board member and Chair of the International Trade Relations committee of the Latin Business Association (LBA) and a member of the World Academy of Arts and Culture.

Lucía has received praise from influential political, community, and business leaders from several countries. She has been a keynote speaker for numerous domestic and international organizations including the State of The World Forum, chaired by Mikhail Gorbachev and Vicente Fox Quezada, the Anthony Robbins Research Mastery University, the Republican Governors Association National Conference, and the World Congress of Women Business Owners.

Her recognition and awards include the Society for Advancement of Management, (SAM) *Millennial 2000 Manager of the Year Award;* Latin Business Association (LBA) *Salute to Hispanic Business* 1998 in Appreciation and Dedication to the Hispanic Business Community; Minorities In Business Magazine, *The Multi-Cultural Prism Award,* and the U.S. Hispanic Chamber of Commerce *International Business Award.*

Ms. De García writes editorials and appears regularly on national and international television, public radio, and in documentaries for the BBC Network and Global Vision

Network LTD. She is profiled in the 1996 Simon & Schuster's *"Latino Success, Insights from 100 of America's Most Powerful Latino Business Professionals."*

Born in Colombia, South America, Lucía De García is multi-lingual and multi-cultural, enjoys reading, traveling, and the fine arts. She resides in Orange County California with her husband Álvaro.

Statements

Ambassador Ananda Guruge, Ph.D., D. Litt. Former Ambassador of Sri Lanka to USA, France, UNESCO, Spain, Algeria, and Mexico.

"What an intellectual as well as emotional treat to read the inspirational life story of Lucía De García whose love for humanity has driven her to highest achievements as a promoter of multicultural leadership for peace and international understanding. She is a veritable bridge-builder among nations and communities. She is so convincing in her appeal for unity and cooperation among peoples that the highest in the country give ear to what she says most eloquently. It is my fervent wish and hope that Lucía will come out in this book as a most desirable role model for all who see our shrinking globe as a home to humanity, rich in diversity and yet united for the achievement of the highest ideals of peace, security, and prosperity."

Jonathan Hutson, Doctor on Jurisprudence Co-author, Bridging the Racial Divide: Interracial Dialogue in America

"Lucía is much more than a savvy international business leader; she provides fresh and spiritual insights as a dynamic Latina voice for interracial dialogue and multicultural collaboration in solving community problems. She understands that at the heart of successful community building, there is love, laughter, and mutual friendship."

Dan Young, Former Principal Commercial Officer, US Consulate-General, Melbourne, Australia, Regional Director, US Travel and Tourism Administration, Sydney, Australia.

"Having seen Lucía De García develop her understanding, appreciation, and capabilities over the years, I can predict her experiences and insights will be an inspiration to many who are beginning their own search for a spiritual ideal to match their aspirations in the multicultural world in which we live."

Maureen Jones-Ryan, Author, Philanthropist, Special Advisor to the World Academy of Arts and Culture

"A moving and inspirational memoir. "Building Bridges" is clearly symbolic of my perceptions of this remarkable book. Thank you for sharing your heart and soul with us through your courageous and self-revealing book. It is like no other memoir or autobiography I've ever read. In my work I meet literally, thousands of women and only rarely do I encounter one of such intellectual curiosity, spiritual depth, and love of life."

Tony Robbins, #1 Peak Performance Success Coach, at Financial Mastery, Arizona 1995

"Love is Lucía's power. Her vision is her vehicle that makes her capture her dream. And with resolve, she is able to accomplish her mission. What a sight of vision! To see countries and people alike! To carry that passion with resolve and with decision, she did not know how, with no means and the resources, she decided and acted until she got what she wanted.

. . . The poetry of describing people and places, those are called magic moments and Lucía seems to capture them regularly. And most importantly, she is able to share them with all."

Dedication

This book is dedicated
To all the women of the world,
To those who came before us,
To Mother Teresa of Calcutta, and others
Who left us a legacy to continue on their path
And make this world a better place.
To those who are transforming our world,
Dr. Jane Goodall, DBE, a Messenger for Peace,
To the emerging women of today
—The Renaissance woman.

. . . And to the men, who with their humility,
their message of compassion, tolerance,
and their quest for unity, justice, and peace
have made an indelible mark in history:
Abraham Lincoln
Albert Schweitzer
Desmond Tutu
Martin Luther King
Mohandas Gandhi
Nelson Mandela
The Dalai Lama

Most importantly,
to my mother, Ana Carolina,
whose spirit still resonates
in every expression,
every place, every moment
of my existence.

. . . and to my grandchildren
Delaney Lucía and Brayden Álvaro
who will carry the torch
of their multicultural ancestors
to achieve an inclusive,
collaborative, and interdependent society.

In memoriam of His Holiness, Pontiff John Paul II,
a Pilgrim, a Fisherman of the Stars, a Wanderer, and
a Bridge Builder between the Vatican and the World,
between God and Humankind.
The Millennial Pope, the Pope for all the People.

–Lucía De García

Table of Contents

About the Author 5

Statements 7

Dedication 9

Foreword 15

Introduction 21

Bridge Builders and Wanderers 25

Leonardo da Vinci's Bridge 27

Part I. FAMILY BRIDGES 29

1. My Journey Begins... 31
2. My Parents 37

Ana Carolina – *Mi Mamá* (My Mother)

Carlos Enrique – *Mi Papá* (My Father)

3. Growing up in Colombia 53

Álvaro – *Mi Esposo* (My Husband)

4. Discovering America 63
5. My Hispanic-American Family – Our Tree of Life: Uprooted, Yet Grounded 75

Grandparents

6. Crossing Bridges Together 93

Part II. BUSINESS BRIDGES 105

7. Élan International 107

8. NAFTA 115

Mesoamerica: Central and South America –
The Andean Condor Meets the American Eagle

9. World Leaders 123

Asia: The Tigers of the Far East –
Marco Polo no Está Solo

10. The High Price of Success 135

Part III. BRIDGES FOR UNITY AND PEACE....... 143

11. Peace Makers 145

A Pilgrimage for Unity and Peace

12. My Life Purpose 169

13. Everything Is Possible: *¡Si Se Puede!* 177

Gracias, Muchas Gracias 185

Bridge Builders of the 21st Century 189

My Favorite Ones 193

Statements of Unity and Peace 299

Index of Quoted Authors 203

About the Cover 205

Foreword

"We have a choice
to use the gift of our lives
to make the world a better place..."

— **Jane Goodall**

"Todos tenemos una alternativa
para usar los dones que nos dá la vida
y construir un mundo mejor..."

I shall never forget the first time I met Lucía De García. It was during one of my lecture tours, and Lucía had agreed to host a luncheon for members at the Center Club in Costa Mesa, California. But the driver who was bringing me from a breakfast engagement got hopelessly lost – we drove for some 20 minutes in utterly the wrong direction! Lucía had to placate all those increasingly impatient people who had snatched precious time from their busy schedules. Eventually the original plan, for me to speak before lunch so that people could talk about what they had heard while they ate, was abandoned and the meal started without me. Therefore, when I finally arrived, Lucía was understandably more than a little concerned.

I was rushed straight to the podium, feeling terribly embarrassed. But Lucía, with the quiet dignity for which she is renowned, gave a wonderful, warm introduction, which made me feel a whole lot better. And so I began my talk. I spoke about the chimpanzees, their plight in Africa as their forests decreased due to human population growth and logging, and due to hunting for the live animal trade and today commercially for food. I went on to talk about the grim conditions faced by humans across Africa and much of the developing world – poverty, hunger, disease, and the pollution everywhere of water, land, and air. And I talked about the inequitable distribution of wealth, the millions of the poor who live on less that $2 per day, the children who die of malnourishment contrasted with the unsustainable lifestyles of elite societies everywhere, the terrible waste that goes on in the developed world. I also talked about the dark times after 9/11. Gradually the knives and forks were laid down and the partially eaten food was left on the plates.

Finally, the fact that each one of us, every day, makes a difference in the world – yet we tend to think that the little we can contribute will not really make a difference. But when we look at the cumulative effect of individual action it is huge.

As always, people responded to this message. There were a lot of questions. Many had ideas as to how they could help. The meals were left half eaten, as people had to go back to their work. I expressed concern that people had left their food, and mentioned the number of poor African villagers it would have fed, not to mention the waste of water in the tall glasses when millions of people have no access to safe drinking water. And after everyone had gone and Lucía and I finally sat down to eat together she went and fetched her own half eaten salad from her table!

We talked and talked about what is wrong in the world and how together we can help to change it. That was the beginning of a special friendship that has grown with the passing of time. Lucía has become one of my staunchest advocates, helping me in countless ways to carry forward the message of hope around the globe.

As a Trustee of the Jane Goodall Institute, Lucía joined me and other board members on a trip to Tanzania to visit the chimpanzees of the Gombe National Park, and our TACARE (Take Care) program in the surrounding villages. Lucía always looks a million dollars. Her clothes are bright and striking, complimenting her lovely face, dark hair and eyes, and her vivid personality. So I could not quite imagine her on this trip. But then, I was forgetting her upbringing in Colombia and her time in the mountains there. She was more than up to the challenge. She even made the difficult climb up to The Peak (where I used to sit, with my binoculars, in the early days).

The mountain is steep and, to make matters worse, Lucía was suffering considerable pain from a back injury– but she did not admit to this until the trip was over. She came with us to four of the 24 villages around Gombe that have benefited from our TACARE program, which improves the lives of people in environmentally sustainable ways. Like others in the group, Lucía was moved by the poverty she saw and impressed by the resilience of the people, their huge and generous appreciation of our efforts to bring more light and dignity to their lives, and to give them more hope for their future.

I watched the warmth with which Lucía interacted with the people and their children, and saw in her eyes the desire to help, to reach out to them in their very different world. This is when I knew that Lucía De García was, indeed, a kindred spirit. Her determination to make a difference – to make indeed the world a better place – is impressive. She is always striving to "build bridges of understanding" between people of different cultures, religions, and political persuasions.

Building Bridges of Understanding is an honest and very moving account of Lucía De García's rich and varied life. She was born into a loving family of unpretentious means in a modest region of Columbia. She shares the problems she faced as she struggled against the innumerable difficulties posed by the social conditions of the South America of her childhood. And we follow her transformation from a loved child to a determined, strong willed and intelligent young woman who sets her sights upon forging a life for herself in the United States of America.

We have one thing in common: Lucía and I both admit the huge influence in our lives played by our families, especially our mothers. Lucía attributes her best qualities – determination, courage, and the capacity for hard work – to her mother. She believes that she herself has become "the embodiment of [her] mother's American dream". We both maintain and draw inner strength from very strong ties to our families.

Recently I watched Lucía with her two grandchildren. They were on their way to a Halloween party, dressed up as a fairy and a prince, and I could see Lucía vicariously reliving her own childhood. Indeed, part of her charm is that she has never lost the essence of childhood – a sense of the wonder and joy in life. It gives her a special innocence that is attractive and very endearing.

This book tells the fascinating story of a passionate, talented and, above all, warm-hearted woman, determined to stay true to her vision, to live out her dream, and to learn all she can from the world around her. The book will surely inspire those who read it and encourage them to follow their own dreams, to live life to the full, take all it has to offer and – most importantly – to give back in full measure.

Jane Goodall PhD, DBE
Founder – The Jane Goodall Institute &
UN Messenger of Peace
www.janegoodall.org

Bournemouth, UK. November 2005.

Dr. Jane Goodall, Ph.D., DBE, is a world-renowned scientist, highly respected for her groundbreaking research of wild chimpanzees and her environmental and humanitarian activism. Among her numerous awards and recognitions are: the United Nations "Messenger of Peace", Dame of the British Empire (DBE), by H.M. Queen Elizabeth II, the French Legion of Honor, and the National Geographic Society's Hubbard Medal. Dr. Goodall spends much of her time lecturing, sharing her message of hope for the future, and encouraging young people to make a difference.

Founded in 1977 **the Jane Goodall Institute,** continues Dr. Goodall's pioneering research of chimpanzee behavior – research which transformed scientific perceptions of the relationship between humans and animals. Today, the Institute is a global leader in the effort to protect chimpanzees and their habitats. It also is widely recognized for establishing innovative community-centered conservation and development programs in Africa, and the Roots & Shoots education program, which has groups in more than 95 countries.

For more information please visit www.janegoodall.org

Introduction

Writing, like life itself, is a voyage of discovery...
The adventure is a metaphysical one;
It is a way of approaching life indirectly,
Of acquiring a total rather than a partial
View of the universe.

The writer lives between the upper and lower worlds:
He takes the path in order eventually
To become that path himself.

— **Henry Miller,** U.S. Author (1891-1980)

Escribir es, como la vida misma, un viaje de revelación...
Una aventura metafísica,
Una manera de acercarse indirectamente a la vida,
De lograr una visión total del universo.

El novelista vive entre los mundos superior e inferior
Y escoge el camino para que se convierta, finalmente,
En el suyo propio.

The idea for this book's theme began to form in my mind a little over a year ago when, in a rather rare moment of solitude, I stood on a high bluff overlooking the Pacific Ocean contemplating a lovely Southern California sunset. As I gazed to the horizon at the vivid red and orange hues of the setting sun, a gentle sea breeze carried to my ears the faint whispers of my ancestors, imploring me from across the ages to pen the words that would chronicle their struggles. It seemed to me significant that their efforts, which had most certainly influenced and shaped my life, would now provide me the inspiration to write this book. Thus, I made the decision to embark upon this story which I hope will serve not only as an enduring testimonial to the trials and tribulations of my forebears, but also as a guide to inspire others to share their life experiences through the written word.

My story should encourage and motivate those who choose to follow the difficult path, a path that leads to understanding cultural differences that divide the myriad peoples of this planet. It is my fervent desire to encourage those who seek this journey to attain the compassion and multicultural knowledge necessary to become "bridge builders" who transform the human face of the Earth as they pursue the challenge of *Building Bridges of Understanding.*

In the northern part of the South American continent, in the Andean Mountains—the longest mountain range in the world—I was born the fifth of eleven siblings. My given name is Lucía Fabiola Giraldo Estrada Botero Vega Restrepo Londoño, a cultural tradition in Latin America designed to instill in us a sense of heritage so we will never forget our roots going back at least three generations.

This narrative contains both humorous and serious anecdotes. It is a reflection of everlasting family and friends' experiences that have always influenced the course of my life. It includes ancient wisdom, poetry, and songs in Spanish and English that still resonate in my heart, chart the course of my life, and sustain me.

There is much I want to share with you, the people I have met in my tireless and frequent journeys across hemispheres, who have transformed my life: world leaders in politics, religion, business, community and the arts. And I especially want to share events that deeply moved me in sacred places that I have visited to pay homage alongside believers, including Cistercian monks, Shamans, Muslims, Hindus, Buddhists, Christians, and Jews — all of whom have contributed to and nourished my spiritual being.

As a woman, an immigrant, a minority by public definition, a Latina or Hispanic, married to a Latino, a mother of two, I faced many challenges in finding the courage to venture into the international business arena and to travel across the world mostly alone to follow my vision. I confronted these challenges over the years, and I finally overcame them. It is far better to explore problems rather than to be paralyzed by them.

Spanish is my mother language and I learned English later in life. While writing this book, the two languages collided at times as I journeyed to the depths of my heart to dig into my feelings and describe my life experiences.

Discovering a new world is an adventure worthy of the many challenges. Some of us think of pursuing our dreams but never make the effort. The reasons are obvious: it requires money, time, and determination. It's not an easy step to take. The uncertainty of a new destination, different cultures and traditions, the strangers you will meet along the way and the unexpected outcomes are part of what you will encounter.

These mysterious elements have driven me to embark upon "the road less traveled" and to discover new worlds. I have been to remote and exotic places, from the north to the south of the American continent, from the Bearing Strait to the Magellan Strait, and across the Americas. From the east to the west of five continents crossing the Gibraltar Strait between Africa and Europe, and sailing the Mediterranean, Indian, China, and the Caribbean seas. To

south and east of the African continent on safaris or visiting secluded villages and mountains to work on behalf of child education programs whose purpose is to preserve the environment and to protect endangered species.

It is a part of my legacy and life's mission to contribute to humanity, to build understanding among people in the hope that they will respect each other's differences and value their shared humanity. This is what people of all cultures must do to reach unity and peace for all.

My multifaceted life has given me the courage I needed to undertake this story-telling mission and it has infused my spiritual walk with guidance, inspiration, and the strength to complete this book.

I am grateful to those who believed in my dreams — my mentors. Those who tried to discourage me – I call my tor—mentors. Finally, to those I met along the way who and contributed immensely to my quest, I say:

!Gracias, muchas gracias!

Bridge Builders and Wanderers

I admire those larger than life individuals who made voyages of discovery by following their dreams. These adventurers came from different countries and cultures, different backgrounds and worldviews, yet each had a clear vision.

—The Genovese Christopher Columbus who sought to establish a permanent sea route to the Orient, and used his persuasion with King Ferdinand of Aragón and Queen Isabella of Castile, to finance his audacious travels. Unfortunately, as with many great men, Columbus's great accomplishment as a discoverer of the "New World" sadly brought much death to the Native peoples of the Caribbean and a destruction of much of their culture.

—The Portuguese Vasco de Gama, a warrior and navigator who discovered an ocean route from Portugal to India by overcoming fear of the unknown and achieving the impossible.

—The Florentine Amerigo Vespucci, a famous Italian navigator who finally recognized that the New World was indeed an unknown continent. North and South America were named after him.

—The Spaniard Bartolome de Las Casas, a Catholic priest, a colonist, scholar and historian. He was called "Defender of the Indians" and was a 16th century advocate of human rights.

—The Portuguese Fernao de Magalhaes, an expert navigator with an impressive military background. He discovered the Spice Islands, what is now Indonesia, during his trips around the world and is usually credited with being the first man to circle the globe.

— The Venetian Marco Polo, a merchant and explorer who journeyed between East and West, and whose writings continue to command our admiration and respect. His writings are widely read even today

— The Scot David Livingstone — "the Pathfinder of Africa" — was a missionary, doctor, and explorer who helped open the heart of Africa to missions and opened the consciousness of Europeans to the unspeakable brutalities of the slave trade. His travels covered one-third of the continent, from the Cape of Good Hope to near the Equator, and from the Atlantic to the Indian Ocean.

— The American Abraham Lincoln for his firm stand on equality and his vital role as political leader in preserving the Union during the American Civil War, and for beginning the process that led to the end of slavery in the United States. He was a man of humble origins whose determination and perseverance led him to the nation's highest office.

— One of South America's greatest generals, *El Libertador,* the Venezuelan-born Simon Bolivar, a warrior, the creator of *El Sueño Americano* and The Pan-American Union.

The lives they led, the things they did and the example they set have inspired me and should inspire us all to explore new dimensions of our humanity.

Leonardo da Vinci's Bridge

In 1502, Leonardo da Vinci designed a graceful bridge with a single span of 720 feet (approximately 240 meters). The Bridge is the epitome of Italian Renaissance art, engineering, and science.

To da Vinci, it was a symbol of inspiration, love and harmony, a union between heaven and earth, the spiritual and the material realm, and for me, that symbol was a beautiful metaphor for the connection among people, cultures, and continents.

—The Norwegian Leonardo Bridge Project
Visit www.vebjorn-sand.com/thebridge.htm

Part I
FAMILY BRIDGES

CHAPTER I

My Journey Begins

It is not where we come from,
It is where we are going that matters.

Lo importante no es de donde venimos,
Sino hacia donde vamos.

— **Abraham Lincoln** (1861- 1865)

Sunrise appeared at midmorning and my mother gathered us to sit outside on our doorsteps to be caressed by the warm sun. Our home was located on the outskirts of the city of Medellin in the foothills of the Andes. We waited anxiously for sunrise. Feeling alone and trapped by these mighty mountains, I looked up at the beckoning world beyond those mountains.

My mother holding me at four months of age

The mountains were my teachers. I always wanted to climb to their highest peaks. As a child, I saw the act of going beyond the next one as a major challenge. They became a symbol of strength and hope, a symbol of my drive to succeed.

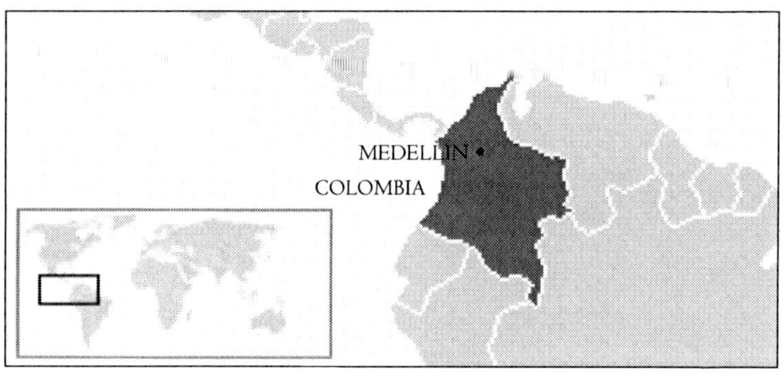

El Canto del Antioqueño

Oh Libertad que perfumas
Las montañas de mi tierra
Deja que aspiren tus hijos
Tus olorosas esencias.
¡Oh Libertad, Oh Libertad!

Al hacha que mis mayores
Me dejaron por herencia
La quiero porque a sus golpes
Bellos acentos resuenan.
¡Oh Libertad, Oh Libertad!

— **Epifanio Mejía,** Colombian Poet (1838-1913)

Hymn of Antioquia

Oh Liberty you have instilled
Your sweet aroma
To the mountains of my native land
Oh do allow your children to partake

Of your most sweet fragrance.
Oh Liberty, Oh Freedom!

To the axe that my forefathers
Bequeathed to me as their legacy
I treasure its exquisite blows
That resonate from its strokes.
Oh Liberty, Oh Freedom!

Medellin, the capital of Antioquia, where I was born, is located in the center of Colombia, in a valley surrounded by the Andes and is one of the largest and most industrialized cities in Latin America. The *Antioqueños* or *paisas* are a fusion of races, ethnicities, social backgrounds, religious practices, and societies. They possess a strong sense of responsibility, a loyalty to their heritage, their region, strong family values, and a deep concern for education and for cultural, and economic progress.

A Multicultural Heritage: Hispanic-European

A mixture of cultures embraces Colombia's heritage.

Spain discovered the area in 1499 and in 1536 colonists and conquerors poured in from Europe, especially from the Mediterranean region, to colonize our regions. Muslims, Jews and Christians from Spain comprised our great Islamic civilization of Al-Andalus–called today Andalusia. They were part of the group of settlers in the *Nuevo Mundo* or New World.

As for my personal heritage, my Jewish ancestors came to the Americas from Spain during the Inquisition. Later my relatives assisted Jewish families who arrived in my hometown in the 1940's when they fled the Nazi occupation in Europe.

My maternal grandmother traced her ancestry to Garcilaso de la Vega, born in Cuzco, Peru in 1539. He was the son of an unwed Inca princess Isabel Suarez Chimpu Ocllo, and a prominent conquistador, Sebastian Garcilaso de la Vega y Vargas. Garcilaso became one of the first Peruvian *mestizos.* He also documented a bi-cultural society in a book entitled *La Inca Florida,* which recounts the origins and rise of the Inca Empire.

Among my ancestors on my maternal side are accomplished authors, poets, intellectuals, and diplomats. On my paternal side, there are landowners, industrialists, and an Army official who fought in the Panama-Colombian War of a Thousand Days.

Colombians inherited several characteristics and gained considerable knowledge from this blend of many races. From our native inhabitants we learned to revere the earth, to defend life, and to preserve nature. From the Spanish Conquistadores we inherited their determination and adventurous spirit, and from our African heritage, the tenacity to work under the most deplorable conditions imaginable.

All these groups combined to knit a profound tapestry of ideas, visions, and thoughts. Today, the people of Latin America are a powerful testimony to the emotional and intellectual struggle faced by this unique mixture of the Old and New worlds, and they are making strides to transform this vast land into a land without boundaries.

Colombia's future is bright as it emerges from decades of lawlessness, hostility, and civil and political unrest. My native country's diversity, combined with my family's history have inspired me to create a multicultural understanding, to bridge the gap that exists between races in our adopted nation, the United States of America, and its different cultures from throughout the world. For the past two decades, I have hosted many gatherings of friends from different countries in my home in California. We exchange food, arts and crafts, and customs, as a way to help each other to adapt to our respective communities. With community leaders, I conduct meetings on how to create a multicultural understanding among us all.

My Parents

Joy is deeper than sorrow.

— **Fredrick Nitzche,** Tysk Philosopher (1844–1900)

La alegría es mas profunda que la tristeza.

Ana Carolina, *Mi Mamá*

"Please, God, send me all the suffering now, so my children will never go through this excruciating agony."

We listened to her plead to the Almighty. At age thirty-eight, Ana Carolina was diagnosed with uterine cancer and at age forty, she succumbed to the disease. The devastating news hit us children hard. The youngest was two, I was fourteen, and the oldest was nineteen. My mother had educated herself while combating the adverse effects of

My Mother Ana Carolina's First Communion

the illness. We would find by her bed the book *On Death and Dying* by Elizabeth Kubler-Ross, which described the five stages of grief and explained this process to us.

The course of the disease was lengthy and painful and took two long, difficult years. My mother was a devoted Catholic and when she was in remission between radiation treatments, we hiked along with her to the top of a mountain which overlooks the city of Medellín. There is a statue, which is a replica of Christ the Redeemer – the statue that sits atop Corcovado Mountain in Brazil. With her debilitating condition, it took hours to reach the top. When we got there, we kneeled down to pray the rosary and asked God to restore her health. These bittersweet rituals went on for several months until her death. Sadly, we all knew that the cancer had advanced. Tragically, neither science nor religion could or would perform a miracle cure.

The last months and days before her death were agonizing. When we returned home from school to confront her suffering and anguish, we didn't know what to expect.

Would we be able to see her one more time, or hear the dreadful news of her final day?

On a Saturday morning before Mother's Day, while we were all in school, we were summoned home to her deathbed. My mother knew she was ready for the long departure and requested her nurses to prepare her.

"Now I am ready. Bathe me; I am leaving on a long journey."

The good-byes were distressing. Surrounded by all her children, our two sets of grandparents, her five brothers and sisters and their offspring, she asked each person for forgiveness, blessed us and exhorted us to lead an honorable life. With the stoicism innate in her, she was ready to depart.

However, at the last minute she uttered a painful cry:

"My children, God, my children, I don't want to die, I cannot abandon them."

This heart-wrenching cry will remain with me for the rest of my life.

We buried her on Mother's Day at the famous local memorial park, *el Cementerio de los Ricos* or Cemetery of the Wealthy, where she took us every Sunday after church to learn about life and death and to admire the sculptures and mausoleums that adorned this artistic resting ground. Hundreds of people of all ages and social strata attended the services, all of whom had benefited from her wisdom and her generosity. She was a friend to all and her message of equality still echoes in our minds. She reminded us continually, "We are all Children of God."

The moral, emotional, and physical responsibilities left to us to share at home with each other were to collaborate in the upbringing of the younger ones, and to obey and be guided by the older ones.

Ana Carolina, raised in a politically aware family was a liberal and a Roman Catholic by her birthright. She was an intellectual, a thinker whose favorite pastime was to sing opera. She played classical music to her children as lullabies. We learned to dance to the beat and rhythm of our African heritage, to play instruments from our indigenous people, and to sing the famous Mexican *corridos* from our relatives in the North.

The works of Alberto Moravia, Albert Camus, Franz Kafka, and others were discussed in her *tertulias* or salons. This exchange of ideas took place in our home several times a month and was attended by the academics of the era. Books such as Leo Tolstoy's *War and Peace,* and Oscar Wilde's *The Importance of Being Earnest,* among others, were discussed as were the burning political and social issues of the day. As a child,

I hid behind the couch in the living room to listen to these conversations. They made an everlasting mark on my intellectual development.

The gifts I received from this early exchange of ideas would later help me to be assertive in my beliefs, to be conscientious in my political choices, to develop a curiosity for world religions, to expand on my readings from the masters, and to develop both an understanding and an appreciation for the music of the world.

"Dios manda a cada hijo con un pan debajo del brazo."

(Children come with a piece of bread under their arms.) was my mother's response when her friends found out she was pregnant.

With the blend of races, we came in every color and shade which made us appreciate diversity. When the subject of our differences came about, she would say,

"Somos como café con leche; algunos nacemos con mas café o leche que otros."

(We are like coffee with milk; some have more coffee or milk than others.)

Her constant advice that we associate with the righteous came through refrains (sayings or proverbs) such as,

"Dime con quien andas y te diré quien eres."

(You are known by the company you keep.)

"Noblesse oblige" and *"Lo cortés no quita lo valiente"*

(If you are courteous and polite that does not mean you are less courageous) was what she would say when we got into trouble with each other or with our friends.

"Cada tejo con su aparejo."

(Birds of a feather flock together.) and

"El que a buen árbol se arrima, buena sombra le cobija."

(He who sits under a big tree will always get the best shade.)

My mother wanted to be a lawyer so she had regularly attended legal proceedings at the courthouse. To a certain extend her dream became a reality when my oldest sister, Marta Lía, entered law school. Because this was very unusual for women in the late 1950s, my mother kept it a secret from my father during the first three years Marta Lía attended the university.

According to my father, women were not supposed to enter higher educational institutions. He wanted his daughters to go to vocational school before we got married. My mother wanted to take my sister to Italy to specialize in Roman law. However, six months before my sister graduated, my mother passed away.

My mother did charitable work at home as a seamstress for underprivileged families. When asked,

"How much do we owe you Doña Carolina?" her response was,

"Whatever you can afford."

These families did not have much money so they paid her modest amounts. With the money she bought more fabric to continue her charitable labor. She sustained the family and assisted her parents and other relatives' in-need.

The mentally challenged found acceptance as well as the less privileged who came to our door to beg for food and clothing. My mother would say,

"Pa' todos hay."

(There is enough for everyone.) and

"Échenle mas agua a la sopa."

(Add more water to the soup) to feed those who came knocking on our door.

On summer vacations, we went to a farmhouse in the mountains to learn to live off the land.

"Cada hoja se mueve solo con la voluntad de Dios."

(Nothing moves without God's will.)

Before sunrise, we would climb the highest peak across the field. Before dusk we could see in the distance a white sheet covering a tree that signaled us it was time to go home. With the help of the major-domos, we chopped eucalyptus trees to build bridges to cross the rivers, took early morning dips in the ice-cold waters, and learned how to deal with the danger of the swift currents and undertows. We milked cows, roasted pigs, went fishing in the nearest pond, planted vegetables, and harvested whatever we required for our daily meals.

These experiences with nature helped us build our character against the elements. To see the fruits of our efforts became an important metaphor for the rest of our lives.

My mother encouraged us to support causes that matched our beliefs, and to participate in events that could change and transform our political system. She was a woman of courage, of conviction and she possessed many gifts. One was a gift for people *(don de gentes)*, a sense of excellence that conquered and achieved the unsurpassed, and a tremendous reverence for all living things in the Universe.

I would like to think that I am the embodiment of my mother's American Dream. From her teachings, I learned to hold life in the highest regard in spite of the many challenges I faced and to turn them into successes. She often referred to a saying related to three things that you should do in life:

"Plant a tree, bear a child, and write a book."

Her exemplary short life on this earth has guided me and given me the will, the tools and the obligation to pass her tradition on to my future generations. In a sense, my life's work has been dedicated to the fulfillment of her vision.

Carlos Enrique Giraldo
Botero at 18 years-old

In my grandfather's time
knowledge of the world was the power.
In this generation
knowledge is the power of the world.

— **Irving Standing Chief**

En los tiempos de nuestros abuelos
el conocimiento del mundo estaba en el Poder.
En la presente generación,
el conocimiento es el Poder del mundo.

Carlos Enrique, *Mi Papá*

My parents met at a church fair where my mother was in charge of raffling a doll. My father followed her, bought a ticket and said, "I want to win the big doll," referring to my mother. That is how our family began. Papá Enrique was a musician and the owner of a small publishing business. In our spare time after we completed our school homework and on weekends, we worked in his shop to earn extra money. We acquired the skills of financial dealings, attained proficiency in grammar, and recognized at an early age that hard work could pay considerably well.

During a time of political chaos, the opposition party that would overthrow the military dictatorship of the mid 1950's commissioned my father to print flyers. One night, the army burst into the few print shops in town. All the disruptive noise woke us up and we quickly changed the color of ink in the machines so they would not find the source of the printed propaganda.

Coming from a matriarchal domestic family structure, my father was a passive force in our household but still embraced our macho culture and favored his sons over his daughters, so his daughters had to keep a certain distance from him. My mother was the decision-maker, the source of strength and spiritual support for our family unit.

When my mother died, we were on our own, without her constant drive and vitality that had sustained us for so many years. In her absence, who was going to make the important family decisions?

Papá Enrique transformed music into a nurturing force for our souls and brought it to the center of our gatherings after my mother's death. Everyone grabbed an instrument to play melodies that brought peace to our mourning. While continuing their education, my brothers assembled a musical group called *"Los Claves."* They performed in private clubs, street fairs, festivals, appeared on television, and ultimately became recording artists.

They graduated from different universities with budding careers in engineering, business administration, performing arts, law, and architecture.

My parents faced numerous challenges in raising their family. With so many children, more than a few suffered the epidemics of the time. When one became ill with typhoid, smallpox, whooping cough, or mumps, the others were bound to get sick as well. During the 1940's, thousands of children were infected with crippling diseases and many did not survive. It was a time of fear and anxiety.

My sister Olga Cecilia was five years old when she was diagnosed with polio. In 1942, there was a worldwide outbreak of Infantile Paralysis or Poliomyelitis. All over town, neighbors informed the authorities when anyone they knew had contracted the disease. The authorities carried away these young children against their parents' will and put them in special sanatoriums to avoid contagious outbreaks. Many were exposed and paralyzed for life. Panic was everywhere!

Exhibiting the symptoms of polio, Olga Cecilia developed a high fever and had no feeling from the waist down. My parents called the family physician and he confirmed the inevitable. With the dreadful news, on a somber night, at one o'clock in the morning, my parents wrapped her in a blanket and took her to a family mountain retreat to hide her for weeks so that she could be treated until the outbreak dissipated.

The only side effect of the disease was that one of her legs was shorter than the other. In the following years, we all took part in the healing process. The therapy consisted of stretching, climbing mountains, and running together so she could integrate back into playing children's games. For years to come, we saw other children disabled for life, wearing braces and walking on crutches. We helped her and we were part of her courageous effort to overcome her disability and to heal!

My oldest brother Jorge "Henry" Enrique contracted meningitis as a child and became a prisoner of his own mind, a tormented soul. My parents treated him differently – he was not pressured to obtain a formal education like the rest of us. Later in life, he exhibited a passion for music and developed into a talented keyboard player and joined my brothers' band. A gifted writer, he described his travels across the country with the inspiration worthy of a great poet. I will never forget his kindness and tenderness especially toward children.

Sadly, drink became his only friend. In 2002, he suffered a terrible car accident that broke every bone in his body, and for a few months, his spirit was destroyed. The doctors told us that Henry would probably die and that even if he survived, he would never walk again. Bedridden, one day he forcefully got up with the aid of a cane and started on his way to recovery. First, Henry took taxis, then buses, and then he walked on his own, step by step. His determined spirit and perseverance helped him survive this tragic accident. He is now walking without assistance. It is a miracle! He has been an inspiration to us all.

On one of my frequent visits to Colombia, my father finally revealed a family secret to me. Ligia Odila, my parents' first-born, a girl, died of pneumonia at age four. One evening he invited my mother to accompany him on a night of music and serenades. Women were supposed to be submissive and my mother refused at first because their infant was sick, but my father insisted and she complied. She died the next morning and he would carry his remorse in silence for many decades.

Now I understand the meaning of his favorite song – one that he played and sang many times in serenades to my mother and to us children.

Silencio

Duermen en mi jardín las blancas azucenas,
Los nardos y las rosas.
Mi alma, muy triste y pesarosa,
A las flores quiere ocultar su amargo dolor.

Yo no quiero que las flores sepan
Los tormentos que me dá la vida.
Si supieran lo que estoy sufriendo,
De pena morirían también.

Silencio, que están durmiendo
Los nardos y las azucenas.
No quiero que sepan mis penas,
Porque si me ven llorando morirán.

— **Rafael Hernández,** Puerto Rican Composer (1892-1965)

Silence

The white lilies slumber in my garden
The fragrant tuberoses and the roses.
My soul, so sorrowful and regret laden wishing
To conceal from the flowers its bitter pain.

May the flowers never know
The torments life has brought to me.
Were they to know pain I feel
Of grief would they too perish.

Silence, for they slumber
The fragrant tuberoses and the white lilies.
May they be shielded from my anguish,
For in my tears will be their death.

We never heard my mother reproach him. However, she usually sang this song to express her pain:

Donde Estás Corazón?

Yo la quería más que a mi vida,
Más que a mi madre la amaba yo
Y su cariño era mi dicha,
Mi único goce era su amor.

Una mañana de crudo invierno,
Entre mis brazos se me murió
Y desde entonces voy por el mundo,
Con el recuerdo de aquel amor.
¿Donde estás corazón?
No oigo tu palpitar,
Es tan grande el dolor
Que no puedo llorar.

Yo quisiera llorar
Y no tengo más llanto,
La quería yo tanto y se fue
Para no retornar.

— **Luis Martínez Serrano,** Spaniard (1900 - 1986)

Where Are You My Dearest Heart?

More than my own life, did I love her
More than my own mother did I love her
I loved her with all my soul
And her love was my only joy.

On a cruel winter morning
In my arms she died
And since then have I lived

With the memories of her love.
Where are you my dearest heart,
I cannot hear your beating heart.
So immense is my pain
I cannot even cry.

I want to cry
But my tears run dry
How endless was my love for her
Now she has left never to return.

CHAPTER 3

Growing Up in Colombia

I Have a Dream Today

I have a dream that my four children
Will one day live in a nation where they
Will not be judged by the color of their skin
But by the content of their character.

— **Martin Luther King,** (1929 - 1968)

Yo tengo la ilusión, de que mis cuatro hijos,
Algún día vivirán en un país donde
No serán juzgados por el color de su piel,
Sino por el contenido de su carácter.

My Family (Back row) Henry and my Father (Second row) Marta Lia, my Mother with Oscar Humberto and Olga Cecilia (Front row) Lucía holding a doll and Iván Darío

There is a saying in Colombia, *"No hay quinto malo"* (The fifth child is always the best.)

As the fifth child in a family of eleven brothers and sisters, I was the one in the middle or the forgotten child. When I was two-years-old, my mother went to run some errands and left me under the care of my two oldest sisters who were five and seven at the time. They gathered their neighborhood friends and played with me as if I were a raggedy doll, tossing me around, shaving my head and applying make-up all over my body. The mockery continued during my childhood. Shy, skinny, and fragile, I was given all kinds of nicknames by my siblings, and I developed an inferiority complex, which made me feel like an ugly duckling.

Additionally, I was left-handed or *zurda* (the wrong way) an aberration in our sub-culture at the time that was considered evil. At school my teacher put me in the center of the classroom. I was mocked and felt like I was a freak in a circus. My classmates were afraid of me and to teach them a lesson, my teacher stroked my left hand with a big stick several times. She aggressively tied my right hand behind my back, mumbled some prayers, and hammered and hit me again. Then she tied my left hand around my back and forced me to use my right hand but to no avail. This kind of punishment lasted from kindergarten through sixth grade and left me with a physical and emotional scar.

Today I am still left-handed and have to deal with the inconveniences of living in a right-handed world, such as opening a door, eating next to someone who is right-handed, using scissors, etc.

In the late 1950s I attended high school at the *Universidad Femenina,* an all-girl semi-private school subsidized by the government. An all-boy school, the *Universidad de Antioquia* was nearby. It was a time of civil demonstrations, similar to the ones that took place in the mid to late 1960s at UC Berkeley. Students banged on our doors and asked us to join them in their struggle against our government. Hundreds assembled in the central park square to hear the speeches of these revolutionaries who became the political leaders of the next decade.

During the riots, the police arrived and used tear gas and fire hoses to dissipate the masses. We panicked and ran, terrified, bumping into each other. Then I heard shots and I saw a close friend next to me fall to the ground with a bullet to his heart. Thousands attended the burial of this student martyr and it marked a turning point for the beginning of democracy in our country. These episodes transformed my life and led me to achieve a better understanding of the political process.

On weekends, young girls would parade up and down the main boulevard while boys stood against the walls delighted with this display of youth and beauty. We wore our best attire, the latest fashions. We wanted to be seen and admired and to get their attention. They regaled us with whistles and compliments. The young men said,

¡Si como caminas, cocinas, me como hasta el pegado!

(If you cook the way you walk, I will eat it all!)

It was during my teenage years that I became more self-confident and it was then when the swan sweetly emerged.

Whenever I go back to Colombia, I become more and more aware that the economic gap is widening: the rich are getting richer and the poor are getting poorer. I occasionally visit my hometown and go to a mountain retreat joined by our extended family of sixty. We gather around the fireplace at night and reminisce about our childhood. We sing songs to the strings of guitars, tell jokes, make paper hot air balloons, and the next morning, we propel them to the sky.

We talk about our formative years' experiences, which make us stronger and bring us closer than ever. There is always a mixture of sadness and melancholy, yet we look back with joy. We all come from the same mother and father; we have all had opportunities along our pathways, but our diverse personalities have created distinct individuals.

The Prophet On Marriage

You were born together
And together shall you be forever more.
But be there spaces in your lives,
And may the winds of heaven dance with you.

Sing and dance as one and joyous be,
But let each one of you to be alone.
As the strings of the lute do separate,
With such music do they quiver.

And together stand,
Yet not too near:
For the pillars of the temple stand apart,
As do the oak and cypress
Not into each other's shadow grow.

— **Kahlil Gibran,** Philosopher born in 1883 in Lebanon

El Profeta en El Matrimonio

Habéis nacido juntos
Y juntos estaréis para siempre.
Pero dejad espacios en medio de vuestra unión
Y que los vientos en los cielos dancen entre vosotros.

Cantad y danzad juntos, y regocijaos,
Pero que cada cual esté a veces solo.
Así como las cuerdas del laúd están solas,
Aunque con la misma música vibren.

Y erguíos juntos, mas no demasiado,
Porque los pilares del templo
Se yerguen separados,
Y el ciprés y el roble
No crece el uno a la sombra del otro.

Álvaro, *Mi Esposo*

My first meeting with my future husband Álvaro was not pre-arranged. The Colombian tradition was that before we introduced a suitor to our relatives, surnames, financial and educational background information on a potential husband was given to them in order for the suitor to be accepted into the family.

Women prepared to become homemakers, good wives and to have children. My parents told me, "Be bright and choose someone who will be a good supporter of the family you are about to start." A woman who was not married by the age of twenty was considered a *solterona* or spinster.

Álvaro and I were students at the School of Architecture and Engineering of the *Universidad Nacional.* I decided to pursue a career and prepare for the future, just in case I ended up alone. Women entering this university at the time were likely to find husbands since there were five hundred men and only seven women.

In 1962, after I completed my admissions test, I went on a tour of the campus with the dean, who happened to be a family friend. I had a portable transistor radio with me as we walked and listened to Latin music. The dean took me to see a gifted student who was working on a detailed drawing. Álvaro was in deep concentration as we observed him through the window. He seemed annoyed with the interruption and

stopped drawing, put down his pencil, looked straight at me, smiled, and swayed to the music. At that moment, I discovered a kindness in his eyes and a great disposition and I knew my future would be with him. My personal quest for the father of my children had just begun and ended!

We both attended several classes, which gave us the opportunity to study together and soon we became romantically involved. Both of us came from all-girl and all-boy schools and it was not the conventional way to date within the university, so we kept our romance a secret from the other students.

Álvaro was born in the 500-year-old historical coastal town of Cartagena. He came from a generation of landowners who had an important import-export cattle firm named *Ganaderia Osorio Hermanos.* Since he was the oldest of three siblings and the only male, they would have preferred that he marry within his kinfolk for the sake of keeping him in the business.

His parents were conservative and traditional. During a school break, Álvaro and I visited them to announce our intention to be married and live abroad. Neither of our families supported our plans. Álvaro came from a different town and my relatives had no idea of his background. Besides, they were not sure he could support a family on his own. Our parents were unbending in their opposition to the marriage. The thought of our new life outside of Colombia worried them. I finally convinced them to allow us to go ahead with our plans by promising that I would support Álvaro in our pursuits abroad. I also said that someday we would return and live near them.

The desire to become independent and to start our own family in a politically and economically free environment convinced us that we were making the right decision. We stood firm about our plans to marry and move to the United States.

Our wedding took place in 1964 during a gorgeous Caribbean sunset at *La Iglesia de Bocagrande,* a church overlooking Cartagena Bay. With the scent of seawater, the sound of the ocean crashing against the rocks, the seagulls flying above as if they were invited to the wedding, we tenderly said our "I do" vows. A lavish reception followed at a private country club attended by over 300 relatives and friends from both families.

One of our wedding gifts was two round-trip tickets to the U.S. for our honeymoon. We interviewed with the U.S. Ambassador in Colombia to apply for student visas. It was a time of quotas, which meant the U.S. government allowed only a specific number of Colombian immigrants to enter the United States per year. We complied with the necessary documents, which included our parent's bank accounts and a letter from them stating that if we were ever in need of assistance, they would take care of us.

During the interview, the Ambassador anticipated that we would not be a burden to the country he represented so he made it easier for us. Even though we didn't ask, he offered us Green Cards. We left the office triumphantly!

This was the first time we had ever ventured outside of our native country, and we were the first of our generation to emigrate to another land. Now ready to visit the United States of America, we left on our honeymoon and embarked on our freedom!

We would be free to raise a family in an environment where opportunities abound, free to choose our political and religious beliefs, and to achieve educational and financial independence.

For us there were no ifs and no turning back. We assured our families of our ability to bear the responsibilities and gave them our word that we would make it on our own. We were firm in our convictions, and in spite of their fears and against their wishes, we left the country with a suitcase full of expectations.

Armed with determination to fulfill our dreams, we said our distressing and tearful good-byes. We stayed in touch with our parents and frequently wrote them letters chronicling our progress. We also sent them photos of our first residence furnished with items that we had purchased with our own money from second-hand stores and garage sales.

Our families were very proud of us when later we announced that we were expecting our first child. They sent us the entire baby trousseau with Álvaro's youngest sister Nancy who was to accompany us on this special occasion. She stayed with us for several years and eventually married an American and raised a family in the U.S.

Relatives visited us every year to learn more about the American way of life. We became role models for our Colombian families and years later, they would send their young ones to study in the U.S. They were proud of our achievements, and we were pleased to serve as a bridge for those who came from Colombia to live in America.

CHAPTER 4

Discovering America

"Two roads diverged in a wood, and I–
I took the one less traveled by,
And that has made all the difference."

— **Robert Frost,** American Poet (1874 - 1963)

Dos caminos se desviaron en un bosque, y yo—
Yo preferí el menos frecuentado,
Y eso marco una gran diferencia en mi vida"

Our first impression of America was that we had to be strong enough to overcome the complexities of living in this immense land or it would consume our existence. We arrived on the east coast in December during one of the worst winters in U.S. history and ended up spending all the money we had received from our wedding on winter clothing. Washington D.C., the

Lucía at the Lincoln Memorial in Washington D.C.

city many foreigners want to visit, was our first stop. Our fascination with this marvelous city led us to tour the political, educational, historical building, and museums. This was how Álvaro and I began our life together.

Knowing little English, but with a great desire to learn about the people of this country, we went on with our lives and faced the daily challenges. We kept our pocket English/Spanish dictionary with us at all times. Even so, there were many times when even the simple task of ordering food became difficult.

On a chilly winter morning, freezing and hungry, I stood at a restaurant counter and asked for a hot chocolate – a very difficult word to enunciate. I tried different ways to pronounce the word but without success. The waiters did not have time to stay with one customer, so I left empty-handed, cold, and disillusioned.

On a hot summer day, I ordered vanilla ice cream and the attendant asked me,

"Big or little?"

I replied, *"frijolito?"* which in Spanish sounds more like beans.

I was elated to be understood until I found out what she thought I meant.

Ordering breakfast at a restaurant was another ordeal.

"Would you like ham and eggs?" the waiter asked.

"How would you like your eggs, sunny-side-up, over easy, or scrambled?

Sausages or bacon?

White, rye, or wheat toast?"

A simple lunch of steak and potatoes would unleash a series of questions.

"Would you like soup or salad?

What kind of soup?

What kind of dressing?

How would you like your steak, rare, medium, or well done?"

We had to make these difficult choices or starve. I could not understand the fast pronunciation of the English language and the hasty pace of the waiters.

Grocery shopping was also a test. There were innumerable staples to choose from, so we survived on bananas, ham-and-eggs, and hamburgers for quite a while until we attained some proficiency in the language.

In the spring of 1965, we decided to go west in search of gold like the pioneers of the mid 1800's. We traveled on a Greyhound bus to sunny Southern California. This trip across country was the first of many we would take over the years to enjoy America the Beautiful.

Looking for an apartment, finding a school to improve our language skills, finishing our education, finding employment, pursuing a career, and learning how to write a resume in English were some of the many difficulties we faced. Álvaro and I began to make friends, first by approaching anyone who spoke our language in a supermarket, a shopping center, or at school.

Our first jobs were opportunities we seized to absorb the culture and adapt to it, to become skilled at earning a living and to become self-sufficient. We were determined to stay in this country and to keep a promise that we had made to each other to raise our family in a society that offered many possibilities.

We became part of the immigrant population competing for job opportunities, housing, and education. I went to night school to learn English. My English skills were poor and I was concerned about not being understood. Our strong desire to adapt and our hope to build a new life in this country gave us the necessary motivation to keep trying.

My first job was in a sweatshop or garment factory in Gardena, a suburb of Los Angeles. A pleasant elderly Mexican woman interviewed me; I was nervous and she sensed that I had no previous experience working in a factory. She asked me in Spanish,

"¿Has manejado una máquina de coser alguna vez?" (Have you ever used a sewing machine?)

"No, pero mi mamá tenía una máquina Singer." (No, but my mother had a Singer machine.)

She laughed openly and hired me instantly. I was paid the minimum wage of $1.25 per hour and gladly took it.

My job consisted of distributing piecework to 200 seamstresses; I had to keep them busy. The few men there were the owners and supervisors and were the only ones who spoke English. These timekeepers were always on our backs with a small gadget that calculated the time it took to produce a certain amount of piecework. There were workers from every nation on the planet of different backgrounds, languages, and ethnicities. I found many similarities with these women, most of them immigrants who came to this country in search of the same dream and with the same desire as mine to provide a better future for their families.

What a wealth of cultures, colors, and dreams!

I never underestimated anyone's potential and I have no doubt that some of those individuals today are helping shape the American continent. It was there that I first encountered the diversity that makes the United States so unique.

I did my job with passion and would have done it in an instant without pay. It was a learning experience and it was the road which embarked me upon my mission to transform this land into a center for leadership in multiculturalism.

It was a crammed workplace with hard-cement floors and barely enough space to move about. There was discrimination among the workers – Latinos were considered the lowest racial group at that time. It became more difficult when I got pregnant. Immediately, I made a promise to give my child every opportunity to get an education and become someone who would succeed in a different environment so she would not have to go through a similar situation.

One year later I was motivated to find a position that would offer a better opportunity for advancement; I found a newspaper ad offering a job as an inspector at Catalina Swimwear, the manufacturer of the famous bathing suits. The pay was an increase of twenty cents per hour and with excitement, I accepted the job. To my surprise, when I arrived the first day, the supervisor took me to a huge table, similar to a drafting board I had used in architectural school. He gave me bundles of bathing suits that I was to check for flaws and take any defective suits back to the seamstresses for repair.

During the following year, I got a job at a large J.C. Penny warehouse in Buena Park earning $3.50 an hour. I counted garments, hung them on iron rods, stuffed them into big boxes, sealed them with tape and took them to the delivery platform to be shipped to stores nationwide. Any task I performed was part of my continuing education. By now, I spoke English fluently and was ready to move one more step up the economic ladder.

Our first years of marriage brought us many challenges. Álvaro found his first job one day when he dropped me off at work. A few blocks away he noticed the Mattel toy factory, the home of the Barbie and Ken dolls, and applied for the night-shift job paying $2.25 an hour supplying parts in an assembly line. I worked the day shift and attended school at night then came home to cook dinner and deliver it to Álvaro by midnight. He arrived home at four a.m., rested for a few hours, and then attended school in the morning.

While searching for another job that would pay more money, Álvaro spotted a newspaper ad that read,

"Looking for a Building Supervisor"

He accepted what seemed to be an opportunity to make progress. It turned out to be a janitor's job, and again, the result of his misinterpretation of the English language. Álvaro quit this job the next day.

Our days were long and the money we made was barely enough to pay for our living expenses. We continued our education but the learning process was demanding beyond my imagination.

Álvaro graduated as a Mechanical Engineer and found a position close to home with the Fluor Corporation (now Fluor Daniels) that took him to unimaginable places across the world on foreign assignments. It was a great break for his professional advancement, for our growth, financial independence, and an excellent opportunity to travel with the family. Now I could stay home and become an American homemaker.

The Álvaro living in America proved that he was capable of taking care of his family. This was so different from what would have happened if we had stayed in Colombia and he had worked under his parents' supervision.

My first child, Lucía Carolina, was born in 1966 on a winter day in Baldwin Hills. After many hours of labor pains and a difficult birth, I was overcome by the fear of being in a strange land and alone. I wanted my husband to give me support at this time, but he was not allowed inside the small labor room. I said my prayers in Spanish and the nurses around me were annoyed.

"What are you saying?" they asked.

"God, please help me!" barely translating word for word in my mind.

The responsibilities I faced as a mother in this new country frightened me.

"What will become of this little one?" I asked my husband, crying.

"What will happen to her if I die?"

"How will she survive in a society with no relatives nearby?"

"Should I go back to Colombia and start a new life there?"

In 1970 on the seventh month of my second pregnancy, I flew to Colombia, taking Lucía Carolina with me while Álvaro stayed working in the U.S. I didn't want to confront these same worries a second time, and Claudia María was born among dozens of relatives who came from different parts of the country to celebrate her birth and baptism with us.

When I returned to the United States with two young children, my life continued to be a wonderful experience. As I integrated my Latin-American culture into the American lifestyle. I was learning more about the U.S. culture, making new friends, volunteering in the community, attending preschool with the kids, and participating in their activities. Now we could afford to buy a house.

In 1974 we moved to Orange County, the Gold Coast of California, the "California Riviera," and the home of some of the world's most popular attractions such as Disneyland. We bought a house in Irvine, one of the nation's largest planned urban communities, and at the time, it was predominantly white. I wanted to belong, to adapt, to incorporate into this society, and I remembered my mother's words,

"Con educación y elegancia no hay puerta que se te cierre."

(If one possesses education and grace, all doors will open.)

"Nunca agaches tu cabeza."

(Keep your chin up), and

"Haz el bien y no mires a quien."

(Kindness is blind.)

We were one of only two Latino families in our neighborhood. My children's Hispanic surname and their dark skinned complexion were targets for those who discriminate against other ethnicities and different racial backgrounds. To my surprise, many years later, when I told my daughters that I wanted to write a book about our experience in the United States, I asked them if they had to put up with any prejudice while growing up. Claudia María told me that she was called a "Mexican beaner" or dark bean, a racial slur toward people of dark color. Proud about her nationality she responded, "I am not a Mexican beaner, I am a Colombian beaner."

These insensitivities never stopped my children from being part of the American culture. Inside our home, we all spoke Spanish, ate Spanish food, listened to our native music, and kept the tradition and the pride of our heritage. Outside the home, the children integrated into the culture that by right was now theirs.

Weary from eating a food different from that of their schoolmates, one day the girls said,

"Mami, Americans eat peanut butter and jelly sandwiches, hot dogs, and Ding Dongs."

"What? What is that?" I replied.

We all went to the supermarket and the girls helped me with the grocery shopping. No more *sancochos, ajiacos, paellas,* and *frijoles con arepas;* now it was time to learn to cook meatloaf, roast beef, baked potatoes, and apple pies.

I often read them the following:

Making Life Better

Standing for what you believe in
Regardless of the odds against you,
And the pressure that tears at your resistance...
...is Courage

Keeping a smile on your face
When you feel you are crumbling
To sustain your fellow man ...
... is Strength

Following the dictates of your heart
Guarantees your resolve
Without losing your way...
...is Determination

Doing more than is expected
So that the unbearable load does
Not overwhelm another without complaint...
... is Compassion

Helping a friend in need
Without concern for time or effort...
...is Loyalty

. . . Holding your head high
And being the best you know you can be!
When life seems to fall apart at your feet,
Facing each difficulty with the confidence
That time will bring you better tomorrows,
And never giving up. . .
. . . is Confidence

Hold your head high
And make your life better every day!

— Unknown

Mantén en Alto tu Cabeza

Firme en lo que tú crees
Independiente de las probabilidades en tu contra
Y resistente a las presiones de tus lágrimas. . .
. . . es Audacia

Conservar la sonrisa en tu rostro
Cuando sientes que te desmoronas
Por sustentar a tu prójimo. . .
. . . es Fortaleza

Hacer lo que te dicte el corazón
Y te lo avale el cerebro
Sin detenerte en el camino. . .
. . . es Determinación

Hacer más de lo esperado
Para que la carga que agobia al prójimo
Le sea más soportable sin proferir queja alguna. . .
. . . es Compasión

Ayudar al amigo en la necesidad
Sin que importen ni el tiempo, ni el esfuerzo. . .
. . . es Lealtad

Mantener en alto la cabeza y dar lo mejor de ti
Cuando parezca que la vida se desmorona a tus pies,
Enfrentar cada dificultad
Confiando en que el tiempo
Traerá para ti mejores mañanas
Sin darte por vencido jamás…
…es Confianza.

Mantén en alto tu cabeza
¡Y haz tu vida mejor en cada día!

— Autor Desconocido

CHAPTER 5

My Hispanic-American Family – Our Tree of Life: Uprooted, Yet Grounded

Branches of the tree of life are they,
Fruits of our seeds.
Their first steps did we help them take,
Will they but help us take our last?

Son ramas del tronco de la vida,
Frutos de nuestras semillas.
Si por nosotros dieron sus primeros pasos,
¿Por que no habrán ellos de ayudarnos
A dar los nuestros en el viaje final?

— Lucía De García

Robert, Claudia María, Álvaro, Lucía, Lucía Carolina and Anthony, Delaney Lucía and Brayden Álvaro

I have traveled with my daughters Claudia María and Lucía Carolina to many foreign lands and spiritual places that have created a sacred bond among us. Our ancestors, the Mayans, the Aztecs, the Incas and the Chibchas were great architects. They built cities, pyramids, and monuments that today represent a symbol of their greatness. We journeyed to these revered places and holding hands, we prayed together for insight into our lives.

This brought inspiration into our lives as a family. Studying and visiting ancient civilizations, patriotic sites, museums, rain forests, and remote villages strengthened our relationship between our past and our present.

Lucía Carolina has a strong personality, typical of a first-born child and she possesses a remarkable discipline and a powerful work ethic. She revealed her independent character at the age of eight when she traveled unaccompanied to Colombia for a summer vacation and had to change planes three times to get there. She asked us for money so she could tip the airport porters and carefully clipped the dollar bills under her skirt.

Lucía Carolina is the one we always go to for advice and stands as a pillar when we discuss our challenges with her. She counsels us to "Never give up and always support each other."

Claudia María, our youngest daughter, has an endearing personality and she possesses a sharp wit. She is the life of the party, friendly, generous, and a free spirit. When she was a child, she could not tolerate being in a confined place such as a playpen, a highchair or a car seat. With exuberant energy, Claudia María would always run around, even on airplanes, which was often an embarrassment to us. Our relationship is great because I identify with her character and free disposition. Even though I had a more conservative upbringing in Colombia, I always gave her the freedom she was striving for. Álvaro and I shared with our daughters the moral principles and strong work ethic we learned from our parents.

As a young woman, Claudia María struggled to find her place in society. She went through a most trying five years with an abusive and difficult relationship that slowly led her to leave the family nest. I pleaded with her not to leave home, and though she tried to end the relationship, her efforts were to no avail. My heart ached as any mother's would, and I was afraid of losing her to a perilous future. In letting her experience a few years of challenges on her own, all I could do was pray.

At a time when we were distant from one another, I persuaded Claudia to accompany me on a vacation to the Yucatan Peninsula to experience the ancient creations of Mexican culture. The Mayan Village of Xcaret is a unique eco-archeological theme park south of Cancun. These pre-Hispanic cities were built starting from a central nucleus where palaces were erected. I felt a need to connect with this early civilization and to explore the sinkholes, magical caves, rock formations, and marine fossils.

Claudia's behavior continued to be distant and aloof. When she was growing up, Álvaro was absent most of the time working on foreign assignments, and I was busy building my company. I was hoping this trip would close the distance between us.

We arrived at the hotel like two complete strangers. There were times when she cried and wanted desperately to go back home to her boyfriend. I tried everything possible to connect with her and make up for the lost time.

On a hot and uncomfortable afternoon, we decided to go to the 1,590-foot underground river in Xcaret to refresh our bodies, energize our minds, and uplift our spirits.

We stood at the bank of the river and put on our life

jackets. Claudia María was anxious to leap into the water, while I felt some reluctance. Filled with excitement, we both jumped into this bottomless river.

Claudia María, an accomplished swimmer, was swimming like a seasoned fish while I was having some difficulty being pulled by the swift currents. The water was freezing cold and my legs and arms struggled to come up to the surface. I was frightened. Seeing my struggle, Claudia María pleaded with me,

"Mami, Mami, let the river carry you. Let go, go with the flow, and do not fight it."

I turned on my back and started to float smoothly. Unexpectedly, I felt a sense of serenity throughout my body. I could hear the melodic sound of the water as my hands touched it as if I were playing a musical instrument. I looked up and noticed beams of light cutting through an opening above illuminating our path, making this river even more beautiful. I steered clear of the rocks that bordered the river and avoided crashing into them.

Along the waterway, there were six different exits where you could stop and relax. If the river got too crowded, there were many attractive places where you could climb out and rest until the crowd eased up. Arrows marked the distance between the exits, directing us to the end.

By now, Claudia María and I were swimming alongside one another, at times holding hands, whispering terms of endearment to each other, and enjoying this natural ride. At that moment, I felt we had crossed a great divide and united our hearts.

Suddenly I realized how similar this experience is to life – taking risks, and jumping into the unknown. It may not be pleasant or comfortable, but we make it better if we act with determination. The light guides us as we gain knowledge and experiences that ultimately give us more self-assurance.

The rocks along the way represented the potential danger within our surroundings. The exits confirmed that if I was tired or felt defeated, there was a way out.

Claudia María will never know the full power of her words on me. Those few simple words helped me recognize one of life's most important lessons: "Go with the flow." I had been in a race to neverland, spending a lot of time making money while along the way, I was in danger of losing the most precious gifts God have given me: my family. My prayers were answered and my child came back home. Now she was ready to stand on her own with hopes of meeting a good and responsible man.

Lucía and Claudia María in the Pyramids of Chichén Itzá, Yucatan

The pace of my lifestyle slowed as I adjusted to family life without Álvaro, who was working overseas. I encouraged my daughters to get an education and to prepare for life, to be careful in choosing the object of their affection, and to find someone kind and dependable, someone who respected us as a family unit, and most importantly, someone who could be a good father to their children.

Claudia María, my "boomerang" child, finally met the man of her dreams. During her studies in finance, she worked at a mortgage company where she met Robert, her boss' son. The next day, Robert came to meet us at our home and I was impressed by his kind and pleasant personality and the respect he showed us. A year later, their wedding ceremony took place at the First Presbyterian Church in Santa Ana, and much like my wedding celebration, we gave her a lavish sunset reception at Orange Hill, overlooking the Pacific Ocean.

Robert comes from a third-generation German, Swedish, and French family and has a background similar to ours in many ways. He was raised in a tightly knit family and a positive environment and supports Claudia María's aspirations. They both work in the financial industry, and are building a solid foundation for their future. They live close to us, and when Robert's family celebrates Mother's and Father's Day, Thanksgiving and Christmas, we are always invited to partake in the celebration. With Robert, we extended our family and gained a son...and a family.

Lucía Carolina is a much different story. She has drive and determination. Serious and studious, she always excels at what she does, whether at school, at her job or at home. She is a good wife and mother and a good friend.

After graduating from Thunderbird University (The Garvin School of International Management) in Arizona, Lucía Carolina brought to Élan International – a company I founded in 1984 – a truly global perspective and the skills of cross-cultural communication. At times, our strong personalities clashed because each of us is compelling, confident, independent, and each of us wants to be the leader in any situation.

My preference was to run a family business and strengthen the family bond. However, like her father, she was driven to be part of a much larger organization. After working with Élan for three years, it was time for her to move on to corporate America.

With excellent skills in the international arena, she got a position with a local medical technology company, which was later acquired by another company located in upstate New York. Lucía Carolina moved to New York and accepted the position as Director of Worldwide Marketing and Distribution. Seeing her leave the family nest marked another stage in our lives. However painful, we encouraged her to pursue her dream.

Lucía Carolina enjoyed her newfound jet-set professional lifestyle which gave her the opportunity to travel to many countries throughout the world. She was able to benefit from her work experience at Élan International and applied it to her new multi-cultural business dealings. I was proud of her accomplishments, which brought us closer together as we shared our experiences in the global market. She continues to advise me on business practices and I will be forever grateful to her.

On one of her frequent visits home, she stopped in Chicago for a business meeting. She phoned me and told me she had met a man in a restaurant. I perceived in her voice that she was excited about him. I asked,

"Who is he?
Is he married?
Where is he from?
You better come home."

The idea that she had met someone from out-of-town alarmed me. Then my mind flashed back twenty-five years when my family had uttered the same words when I met Álvaro.

Anthony Michael was born in Ohio, lived in Kentucky and worked in commercial banking; Lucía Carolina was born in California, lived and worked in New York. Being from different cultures, what kind of relationship could they have? Would Tony understand our deep-rooted Hispanic culture?

They talked on the phone every evening and saw each other every three weeks. I became more understanding about their relationship and three months later, he visited us in California and asked us for her hand in marriage.

His personality is enticing. He comes from third-and-fourth generation German, Swedish, and Irish backgrounds. His work ethic is similar to Lucía Carolina's, and they share a great sense of responsibility and ambition.

The preparations for the nuptials began with our visits to Ohio to meet his family and friends. During the summer of 1998, Lucía and Tony celebrated their wedding at the Meridian Hotel in Newport Beach, officiated by a Justice of the Peace, even though we would have preferred that they marry within our religion.

More than 200 relatives and friends attended; people from her childhood days through college, people she worked with and met in her travels, and some from distant parts of the world. We danced to the music of an Andean group playing South American songs.

The festivities went on for three days from a sunset cruise in the Newport Beach islands the day before, to a morning of golf for the men. The morning after the wedding, we had a Mexican brunch in San Juan Capistrano. It was a multi-cultural celebration as we began to acquaint ourselves with our new family.

In the beginning, the cultural differences between us had not yet surfaced. It was only after they started their lives together that our idiosyncrasies started to emerge. Our intense Latino personalities, our frequent visits to keep the family together, and speaking a language Tony did not understand, seemed to overwhelmed him. Álvaro and I rushed to their side when their first-born arrived because we wanted to bond with our grandchild, which is an important part of our cultural tradition. Lucía Carolina asked her father to stay with them in the Midwest for the first year of the baby's life.

Álvaro chose to retire from work early in life to nurture the new family and make up for the years he had been absent. He did the same when their second child arrived. It is with misty eyes that Lucía Carolina shares these special moments in her life with her friends.

Much to our delight and pleasure, a Catholic ceremony was performed in Ohio with the attendance of their first baby and Tony's relatives. This was a testimony to her religious upbringing and a bequest to their children. I had written the following to them on their wedding day.

Dear Lucía Carolina and Tony,

This is an exciting time, with unknown adventures and shared experiences. You make us very proud. To continue in the tradition of a culture we inherited from our ancestors, is a step to a brighter future.

For Álvaro and me, it is the result of the education, discipline, and values we instilled in you; for this, your children will be grateful.

Make the most of each passing day, for it is precious.

Treasure every moment and store it in your memory.

Congratulations!

As a wedding present, I gave Lucía Carolina the book The Prophet by Kahlil Gibran with this dedication:

My dearest daughter,

May you read these pages carefully, and only when you are in the quietness of your life. May these words bring to you the understanding we all seek for in our lives, and may you understand, why today, more than ever, I feel free.

May you have the blessings that the universe presents to you...

I have finally begun to comprehend its vastness and the meaning of why I stand alive today.

With all my love,
Mami

We instilled in our daughters the principles and values of self-reliance, respect for the environment and other human beings, and the universe. We were holding them accountable for building a better generation than that of their parents'; after all, they had been born in the United States of America where new opportunities abound.

Lucía Carolina and Claudia María have assimilated into both cultures, the Hispanic and the Anglo, and speak English and Spanish fluently – gifts that will always make them appreciate their heritage, maintain the ideals and traditions of their ancestors while integrating into another culture. Our sons-in-law, Tony and Robert have made an effort to learn Spanish. Their families have given us a better understanding of our new intercultural relationships, while appreciating our differences.

For years, I shared with my daughters books, poems and wisdom, as my mother did with me. There is one book in particular that I treasure. *The Four Agreements* by the Mexican author Don Miguel Ruiz is rooted in traditional Toltec beliefs. These are essential steps on the path to personal freedom:

1. Be impeccable with your word. Speak with integrity. Say only what you mean. The word is the most powerful tool humans have.

2. Do not take anything personally. Self-importance leads people to think they are the center of the universe, causing pain and injustice.

3. Do not make assumptions. To avoid frustration and blame, ask what is meant.

4. Always do your best. This is the surest way to avoid self-condemnation, but never forget that one's best is always changing.

Grandparents

El Nieto

Mi carne, que comienza a sufrir el invierno,
Renueva su esperanza nacida en otro cuerpo.
Sobre el abismo ancho que los años abrieron
La hija – bello puente – me abre camino al nieto.

En mis brazos cansados dormidos lo sostengo
Y es como si llevara una canción en peso.
La vida que yo di ahora es dada en renuevo;
No soy yo quien la dá sino lo que más quiero.

En mis brazos mecí ayer mi flor de almendro;
Al fruto de esa flor ahora lo estoy meciendo.

— **José María Souviron,** Poeta Español

The Grandchild

My flesh, that begins to suffer the winter,
Renews hope through birth in another body.
Spanning the gaping abyss opened wide by the passing years.
My daughter – shining bridge –
Opens for me the way to a grandchild.

In my weary arms does he gently sleep.
As if a lighthearted melody I do bear.
The life I gave is now renewed;
That precious gift was not from me,
But from the one I love the most!

Proud Grandparents Álvaro and Lucía
With Brayden Álvaro and Delaney Lucía

In my arms my almond blossom did I cradle yesterday
And now its fruit I gently rock.

One of grandparents' most important obligations is the passing of wisdom and family history to grandchildren.

Tony and Lucía Carolina's children have made us the happiest *abuelitos* on earth. Delaney Lucía and Brayden Álvaro were born in Loveland, "the Sweetheart of Ohio." We visit them four times a year and they come to California to celebrate *La Navidad* (Christmas) with us and learn about our Christmas rituals. It is a wonderful way for them to stay connected to their Hispanic heritage. We teach them prayers, songs, and games we learned as children; dance with them to the Caribbean beat, cook Latin American food, and speak to them in Spanish. All of these activities are important so that someday when they visit Colombia, they will not be strangers to our traditional roots and our relatives.

Our grandchildren are the new citizens of an ever-emerging world civilization. They have inherited diverse cultural traits from their ancestors plus an exotic mixture and wealth of colors and languages.

I cannot help but wonder what their next generation will be like as these multi-cultural relationships evolve.

A Celebration of Love

Ne marche pas devant moi, je peux ne pas suivre.
Ne marche pas derrière moi, je peux ne pas mener.
Marchent près de moi et soient juste mon ami.

— **Albert Camus,** French Novelist, 1957 Nobel Prize for Literature, (1913-1960)

Don't walk in front of me; I may not follow.
Don't walk behind me; I may not lead.
Just walk beside me and be my friend.

No camines en frente de mi, no se si te seguiría.
No camines atrás de mi, no llevaría la delantera.
Camina a mi lado y seamos amigos.

Our first 20 years of life in the U.S. were difficult. Álvaro was away from home for long periods and we became strangers. I was bringing up our daughters with all the responsibilities of a single parent, and building a business of my own against his wishes. These events made us uncomfortable with each other.

Adapting to a culture so different from ours, re-educating ourselves, and going through that painful process was another challenge. I missed my country, its idiosyncrasies, and most of all, the loved ones I had left behind. My grandparents, my father, my youngest brother Sergio Alfredo, whom I adored, died within the first ten years of my departure from Colombia. I wanted to attend these private ceremonies, but the responsibilities with my children and the economic situation prevented me from traveling to Colombia.

We had questions that we struggled with over the years:

Where do we belong?

Again, the feeling of *"No soy de aqui, ni soy de alla"* (I don't belong here, nor there) a phrase used by many of us about the frustration of living in another land emerged.

We finally realized that our home was in the country of our affections, the one that had nurtured us in democracy and freedom, the nation where our children were building their future and their children's future.

Was it time to go back "home" to our birthplace?

Or was the United States, the country that adopted us so many years ago, the place where we would spend the rest of our lives?

The gap between the North and South American continents became wider for us. We had learned the "system" and the American way of life. Moreover, the United States was the gateway to the rest of the world, and we, as U.S. citizens, could travel to foreign countries more easily.

Álvaro has finally settled down after many years of traveling. We have now been married for more than forty years, a major achievement. We are in the autumn, twilight, and sunset of our lives. Our children have long since left the nest, our responsibilities have lessened, and now we nurture each other and our families at a distance.

Despite the everyday difficulties we encounter, the real meaning of our relationship is the peace we find in the deepest part of our beings, the intimate place where neither one of us chooses to lie or deceive. We recognize that the backbone of our life together is the real love, the true love for which we have always reserved a place in our hearts, although there were times when we feared that it had vanished.

CHAPTER 6

Crossing Bridges Together

Caminante no hay camino,
Se hace camino al andar.
Y al volver la vista atrás
Se ve la senda que nunca
Se ha de volver a pisar.

— **Antonio Machado,** Spanish Poet (1875-1939)

Wayfarer, there is no road,
But the one you make as you venture forth.
And a glance behind reveals the path
That never shall you tread again.

Marital Devotion

After years of traveling across the world, sometimes on family vacations, other times on separate job assignments, my husband and I decided to take a different trip, a trip of freedom. We wanted to fly and soar now that we

Lucía crossing the Capilano Bridge in Vancouver, BC

were unburdened of all the weight we had carried over the years. The time had come for us to become more familiar with America, the adopted country we had come to love.

America has great depth and breadth geographically and historically. America's history is important to us and its natural wonders are captivating. To visit the place where the Pilgrims landed, to see the Civil War battlefields and to walk on the trails pioneered by explorers from other countries was a dream we both shared. It was time to explore the North American continent.

In the early summer of 2003, we made an important decision. As much as we loved our home in Irvine, we decided to sell it. This was difficult because this was where we had raised our children. We listed the house for sale and two days later, embarked on a cross-country journey.

We packed up our SUV, a comfortable gold Infinity QX4 with the simple necessities for a few months of travel and took off on the adventure of our lifetime. With AAA maps, we plotted our fabulous journey. From Southern California up the west coast, to Western Canada, then across the northern states up to Eastern Canada, down the east coast, across the southern states, and back home.

What resulted was an unexpected discovery of our souls, a celebration of our love, and a renewal of our marriage vows. Little did we know when we started that we were about to rediscover attributes and qualities about each other along with problematic behaviors.

Álvaro is an introvert. He never expresses his feelings and most of the time I have to guess what is bothering him. His silence is his reproach. Álvaro lives in the past, not realizing that Colombia and its people have evolved, and he still believes to this day that women belong in the house.

In all our years together, we had struggled for power. The

first 500 miles of our trip were quiet, anxious and before we knew it, it became a competition for power and domination. The "macho man" syndrome was reflected when Álvaro took control of the wheel. I pleaded with him for hours to let me drive but he refused.

By the time we arrived in Portland, I had had enough! Álvaro was in charge of making all the decisions: where to eat, stop, or sleep. At one point, when he was distracted, I moved into the driver's seat and grabbed the wheel.

At last! Now it was my turn!

I drove the next two hundred miles aggressively, speeding with my eyes fixed on the road. I had waited a long, long time to do this. Álvaro was livid but did not utter a word. Was it the fear that if he said something wrong he would never hear the end of it from me? Whatever it was, I would not yield this time. Finally, he broke his silence.

"Stop," he said, "I am getting out. Take me to the nearest airport. I am going back home."

I did not respond but continued driving, looking straight ahead. "Stop!" he demanded. "You can continue your trip alone if you want."

The next few minutes seemed like an eternity. I was tempted to go on my journey alone, but was I ready? I realized how obstinate we both had been. It was going to become The War of the Roses if one of us did not give in. At that instant and quietly, I offered him the wheel as we continued to Seattle without uttering a single world.

We visited museums, grabbed some food at the Fish Market and had cocktails and dinner by the bay. When we reached Vancouver, Canada and after walking in the Museum of Science, I finally broke down in tears.

"Álvaro, I can not take it any more, I am not feeling well," I said.

I was suffering from Lupus, a chronic illness that I had concealed from everyone including him. Systemic Lupus Erythematosus, SLE is a chronic, inflammatory, potentially fatal autoimmune disorder. My body was signaling pain, fatigue and even exhaustion, though my mind and spirit were stronger than ever. My heart was aching because I had been trying to keep this relationship going for so many years for my children's sake! He had been gone too long and too often on foreign assignments and I had become more independent.

We sat quietly for about an hour just looking at each other; he could find no words to express his concern nor could I find a way to express the vulnerability I felt. Silently we intuited that we both needed and wanted to continue this life journey together.

It was here and now… or never!

We renewed our vows, the precious and eternal promises we had made to each other when we were in our 20's. The words "in sickness and in health, till death do us apart," came alive with a renewed vitality for both of us.

We continued on our Canadian trip. Though we exchanged few words, we both felt a serenity descend upon us. We traveled by ferry and watched whales and dolphins entertain us with their water dances. We traveled to the sophisticated city of Victoria, British Columbia's capital city. We toured the city on a horse-drawn carriage, had afternoon tea – English style – at the famous Fairmont Empress Hotel, and drove to the stunning Butchart Gardens outside the city where we had a picnic.

By now, Álvaro and I were becoming friends again. We started to share all the untold stories of our trips away from home, interesting people we had met and places we had seen. We enlightened and entertained each other.

It was early morning in Vancouver. We went across the Lions Gate Bridge to the world-famous Capilano Suspension Bridge, 450 feet across, and 230 feet above the Capilano River. I tried to walk the bridge alone as I had crossed so many bridges in the course of my travels, but unexpectedly, I became apprehensive and as I started to turn back, Álvaro lovingly offered me his hand to take me across.

As the scent of the morning dew filled the air, serenity invaded my soul, and with anticipation, I accepted him. In the course of our lives together, I had always acted as if I could stand alone, but now I let go as we walked slowly on the unsteady path as if bridging a chasm, a moment which marked the beginning of our reconciliation.

Walking through gardens, crossing rivers, hiking up mountains, and strolling in the park were symbolic acts to bind our past to our future together. We re-structured the foundation of our relationship and established a solid base for our family.

We were relieved of the heaviest burden, *"la cruz del matrimonio,"* or the heavy cross of marriage, as our Catholic upbringing instructed us before we got married. But to do so, we both had to forget our grievances, reach beyond our arrogance, and realize that if we wanted our children to build a strong foundation for their lives, we had to set the example.

What had we missed all these years?

Could we revive the love we thought was gone?

To begin again became easier; romance knocked on our door, and we chose to let it in. We enjoyed every instant of this passageway to our hearts.

I found that Álvaro was who I thought I had married, the man of my dreams. The great qualities I had seen in him when we first met had reappeared and I started to appreciate them once again. Álvaro is kind, solicitous, and dependable, not only with our family, but with everyone else as well.

We drove peacefully and comfortably along the wild scenic Missouri River, a region Lewis and Clark first explored. Yellow Stone National Park is an area once rumored to be "the place where hell bubbles up." We spent two days contemplating and revering the dynamism of the geothermal wonders, the geyser basin, watching eagles fly above, and buffaloes, bears, gray wolves, and deer graze in the grass. Here was Nature in all its splendor.

We wanted to revisit Chicago where we had lived in the early 1970's during Álvaro's two-year job assignment with Fluor Daniels, but then we realized we were only a few hundred miles away from our grandchildren's home near Cincinnati, Ohio. It seemed that it would take forever to get there, and we recognized where our hearts belong and where "home" is.

Mi Pueblo Natal

A lo lejos se ve mi pueblo natal.
No veo la santa hora de estar allá.
Se vienen a mi mente bellos recuerdos,
Infancia que yo nunca olvidaré.

Ya vamos llegando, me voy acercando.
No puedo evitar que los ojos se me agüen...

— **Jairo Varela,** Colombian Musician (1949 -)

My Hometown

At a distance lies my native land.
That I can hardly but contain
My fervid anticipation to be there.
Precious are memories that engulf my mind
Of a childhood never to forget.

We are almost there, as I draw near
I cannot hold the tears that fill my eyes...

Just before midnight we arrived at their home. Lucía Carolina, Tony, Delaney Lucía, and Brayden Álvaro were waiting anxiously for us outside. With the help of their parents, the children drew in the driveway a large map of the United States showing the route we had taken from California right up to Loveland. Feelings of happiness invaded all of us.

We spent a couple of weeks with our grandchildren attending school events, walking in the parks, visiting the zoo and children's museums.

The gap among our different cultures was broad, not only the Hispanic and the Germanic, but also the Californian and the Midwestern. On this visit, we continued to strengthen our Hispanic culture.

There were no tears when we said our good-byes. Instead, we were in high spirits and grateful that we were able to spend quality time with our grandchildren.

As we continued on our journey, we phoned the children, told them where we were and sent them postcards from our many stops along the way.

We drove northeast, bound for Detroit, Toronto, Niagara Falls, the Finger Lakes in upstate New York on seemingly endless highways, surrounded by thousand of dense towering dark-green-leafed trees. Eventually we reached Newark, New Jersey on the Hudson River. There we stood at a monument built in memory of the victims of the World Trade Center Towers in Manhattan.

We left the car in New Jersey, crossed the mouth of the river by ferry to New York City, and spent a day reflecting and paying our respects to the victims of the terrible tragedy at Ground Zero.

Could we have done something to prevent this disaster? I wondered. I reflected on how much our world needs unity and peace.

We continued to Virginia where our nephews, Germán José and Augusto Enrique and their families now live and spent hours reminiscing about our visits to Colombia when they were growing up. We celebrated together the Fourth of July in Washington D.C. at the Mall in front of the Capitol.

After a few days with them, we continued our journey driving through the Shenandoah Mountains Ridgeline in Virginia. After hours of the most breathtaking landscape, driving on narrow twisting roads and through quaint towns, we reached this magnificent palace, The Homestead Resort. Built in 1766, this 15,000 acre spread in the middle of the Allegheny Mountains in Hot Springs, Virginia is a historic monument and has been a destination for many presidents.

With a Romance Package we celebrated our 40th wedding anniversary and stayed in a suite in the Clock Tower overlooking a superb view of the Cascades golf course. With tea on the terrace, elegant dinners, spring baths, spa sessions, horse carriage rides in the woods, and hikes in the forest, Álvaro and I sealed our pact of personal unity and peace.

It was here in this charming place where we experienced a magical moment during an elegant champagne dinner. I noticed that Álvaro was unusually quiet. With a special look and misty eyes, he uttered:

"I have never known happiness till now."

Wanting to cherish this moment, I gently touched his hand. It had taken him all these years and the serenity and solitude of this place to appreciate the meaning of love.

We traveled south with stops in the historic towns of Savannah, Georgia and St. Augustine, Florida where we took tours through the old districts' attractions that bring to life the history, adventure, and romance of the Old Cities.

We had now crossed almost 8,000 miles by the time we arrived in Miami. Our Osorio relatives who had moved from Colombia a few years ago invited us to stay with them. Together we took a drive to the Florida Keys and stood in the southern most part of the United States where we could see the lights of the island of Cuba ninety miles off shore. A number of Cubans have risked their lives to cross to our shores for what they consider the American Dream.

We continued driving on mysterious roads throughout the night along the Florida West Coast and along the Gulf of Mexico. By dawn we reached one of our favorite destinations: New Orleans. To make up for the long, tiring drive, we chose to stay at a chic hotel in the historic riverfront district. On a hazy morning we had coffee with pastries and from our balcony watched cruise ships depart for the Caribbean. In the afternoon we stopped at an old plantation and then took a diner cruise up the Mississippi River.

Later, a stroll through the French Quarter brought us to a palm reader who envisaged a bright future together filled with many exciting adventures.

Now we pray for the rebuilding of this marvelous historic and musical home, and the healing of the thousands of people who suffered from the devastations of Katrina in 2005.

We arrived in Austin where our niece Eileen and her family reside and spend a couple of days strengthening our relationship and bonding with their young ones.

It was August and the sun was getting stronger in the south; the temperature reached 120 degrees. We decided to continue our journey and drove through desert storms in the states of Texas, New Mexico, Arizona, and California, with occasional stops to visit other relatives and friends. It was 80 degrees when we arrived in beautiful and sunny Southern California.

On our cross-country journey we had learned a great deal about each other. All through married life, we had struggled and made sacrifices. Now there were no more disagreements and the rivalry had finally subsided. We had shared experiences never before imagined, discovered great qualities about each other, and recognized and respected our needs and desires.

The heartfelt conversations continued on a daily basis about the many places we had visited. This journey was truly a gift we had given to one another physically, emotionally, and spiritually.

On this trip we experienced the America we had dreamed of when we were growing up in Colombia.

After traveling 11,500 miles in two and a half months, we finally returned home. By now our house was sold. We had only a week to dispose of the unnecessary stuff and move to a new residence. Then we began to build our new home in the same area. We remodeled it, selecting artifacts and possessions most precious to us and art collected from years of traveling to more than sixty-seven countries. This would be our final destination.

One morning I heard a loud crash; I ran downstairs imagining a terrible disaster had happened. Álvaro had been downstairs unpacking boxes in the garage; frantically I looked for him fearing he had fallen. Instead, I found scattered on the marble floor hundreds of small pieces of four of our precious Lladro porcelains. For years I had been collecting the figurines that represented Romeo and Juliet, Othello, the Venus de Milo, and Don Quixote and had been saving them for my daughters.

Bending on the floor I started to gather legs, hands, heads, and torsos, and my immediate reaction was to run upstairs to my sacred place, an altar I had long ago assembled with icons inherited from my grandparents and my in-laws. I visit this place frequently to thank God for our blessings, and pray for those in need. It gave me a great sense of peace and appreciation to find that Álvaro was unharmed.

My husband has been a rock of Gibraltar with his continuing love and devotion to our family. He is now involved and supportive in all of my business and community activities, but most of all, he is a wonderful friend who allows me the freedom to be and do what the inspiration in my soul desires.

Grow old along with me,
The best is yet to be.

— **Robert Browning,** English Poet (1812-1889)

Permanece por siempre a mi lado,
Lo mejor está aún por venir.

Part II

BUSINESS BRIDGES

CHAPTER 7

Élan International

Whatever you can do
Or dream you can, begin it.
Boldness has genius,
Power, and magic in it.

— **Johann Wolfgang von Goethe,**
German Philosopher (1749 - 1832)

Todo lo que desees hacer
O sueñes que puedes hacer, empréndelo.
La valentía tiene genio,
Poder, y magia.

The Beginning of Élan International
Lucía in 1984

By 1975, Álvaro's income supported us with a comfortable lifestyle and provided the security for our children's education. However, I wanted my own career, to be prepared for the future, and to be capable of meeting any challenges or uncertainties my family might face. I was determined to become a professional businessperson and incorporate into the mainstream.

With a background in architecture and engineering, I was ready to find a better job, an occupation where I could use the training and competence I had gathered over the past decade. A firm in Newport Beach hired me as an Engineering Designer at the *incredible* salary of $5.50 an hour. Men doing the same job were paid $10 hourly. There was no Equal Opportunity Employment for women or minorities at that time so I was afraid that if I complained, I would be fired. I was the only woman in a company of 300 employees in technical engineering.

International politicians and entrepreneurs often visited the company. I was involved in various world projects and attended meetings where I was able to share my expertise in business protocol, a great way to demonstrate my knowledge of cultures and the experience I had gained from visiting other countries.

This company was doing business abroad but lacked the cultural sensitivity to deal with these countries, which caused them to lose numerous projects. The need I saw for cross-cultural communication and the widespread inability to understand new cultural behaviors prompted me to go into business on my own.

I came to the United States because I saw it as a place to be creative and a place where I could leave a legacy to future generations. My hope was to start my own business so I could contribute, be industrious, and ultimately be successful. I also faced challenges, and more importantly, I knew I had to overcome them to achieve personal success and balance among my family, my career, and my community. This is what epitomizes "the American Dream."

I was motivated to go to new heights. In 1984, I started

my own business as a sole proprietorship in a small corner of my home. Later it became a California corporation.

Was I prepared? Yes.

What was my next step?

To dare to do what seemed impossible and pursue my mission.

What gave me the courage?

I recognized that this enterprise required basic skills and tenacity, and that success is a voyage, not a destination.

Trailblazers and entrepreneurs do not do what everybody else does. My husband discouraged me and friends predicted that I would never last. I knew it would take money, hard work, persistence, and patience among other things, but I was determined to succeed, and never to give up what I had just begun.

As Los Angeles prepared for the 1984 Summer Olympics, I worked on a volunteer committee to host Latin American athletes, work that gave me the confidence to start my consulting firm.

I needed a partner so I called my best friend and confidant, Diane Diehl, now a protocol consultant, and together we embarked on this new endeavor. Diane and I had participated in charitable organizations and were successful in planning events for museums, the performing arts, and repertory theaters. By volunteering at many levels, I had also contributed significantly in building relationships between the community, business, political, educational institutions and the arts in Southern California. As trustee for universities and community-based organizations such as the American Red Cross, I had all the necessary components to do well.

The first step was to name the company. Diane and I came up with "García & Company" and "García Enterprises," but we decided it sounded too ethnic and at that time in California, it would not work. It had to be unusual and elegant. Therefore, Élan International was born.

In French élan means impetus, vigor, spirit, and doing things with style. In Latin, it means to throw a lance, a way of doing things with force, spontaneity, and always with enthusiasm. In English élan means energy, imagination, style, and flair. Perfect!

Our first targeted project was the 1984 Summer Olympics in Los Angeles; after all, it was in our own backyard. The International President, Juan Antonio Samaranch was from Spain and we headed for Europe to meet him. Putting the final touches on the Élan brochure at the airport, Diane and I were on our way with our portfolios full of photographs and newspaper clippings, exhibiting our community involvement.

Diane and I arrived in Madrid armed with high expectations and optimism. After several attempts to meet with different government officials, we finally went to see the Minister of Foreign Relations. We entered an impressive office and behind the desk, we saw a distinguish man with a kind smile. He asked us to sit down and said,

"So, what can I do for you ladies?"

We looked at each other somewhat bewildered by our ability to reach the top. He listened to our story, how we started the business, and our desire to collaborate in protocol with the Olympic Games. Perplexed and looking intently at us, he stated,

"My dear ladies, there is an office in San Francisco, California that represents the International Olympic committee and those are the people you need to see."

We left the building disheartened and acknowledged how naïve we had been, sat on a bench at a nearby park to meditate and plan what to do next. The following days we visited art museums, churches, and savored the culture and the traditions of this amazing country, *La Madre Patria*, my ancestor's fatherland.

With Élan International, the economic opportunities were immense. I attended college to study small business administration and pursued this venture with passion.

There were advantages and disadvantages to being a woman in the international arena. The disadvantages were traveling in foreign lands alone, leaving family responsibilities, and recognizing the lack of women in this field. I had competitive advantages: a pioneering spirit, an understanding of cultural differences, my cultural background, and the idiosyncrasies of my birth country.

If one has the skills, language abilities, and is capable of meeting the needs of the international consumer market and client, it is a win-win situation. By making Élan work from concept to reality, protocol in business was born!

Bridging corporate America with countries in development was a natural for me. Despite the obstacles usually faced by women in business, I found myself at the head of an international venture that specialized in creating opportunities between corporations on both sides of the border. It was a "one-stop" business center for companies needing advice, government permits or other services to set up shop in foreign countries.

The American business attitude is quite efficient when dealing at home, but very naïve and full of preconceptions when doing business abroad. Many companies have a problem with business protocol. For example, in Latin America, business meetings begin with small chitchat, and Americans find that such sociability is a waste of time. To Latin Americans, starting abruptly and moving directly into business dealings strikes them as cold-hearted; it makes them feel uncomfortable.

People think that culture is only food, dress, and arts and crafts. How you motivate your foreign clients is largely determined by their culture. It is important to use consultants who will take charge of social and professional introductions and connections. While language and protocol are in a way related, I intended for Élan International to bring them closer together: to create understanding between businesses in all countries.

I was a rare species, a female president of a company which I had not inherited by marriage or by birth. My vocation was to contribute to other people's progress, and I wanted to fill that void. All of these characteristics helped me transform my desire to succeed and make tangible accomplishments.

The first year I made $2,500 and to survive in my business I borrowed money from my husband who had a successful job. However, I didn't have his emotional support. He was afraid I would lose my dedication to the family. I continued with my struggle to stay afloat in my business. After a couple of years, Diane decided to stay home and take care of her two small children. I was saddened but continued to work by myself to reach the goals we had created together.

A few years later, my daughter Lucía Carolina earned her Masters Degree and became part of my business. We moved into a cubicle in Newport Beach and began restructuring the company. Working closely, we both knew that there was no other way but up; the sky was the limit. We took the next step for expansion, refinanced our home, and moved to a high rise building in trendy Fashion Island, a financial center of the West coast.

From our elegant offices on the 11th floor, overlooking the Pacific Ocean, and on a clear day, seeing Catalina Island, I felt trapped. Occasionally, I gazed at this magnificent view and recognized that looking out at this world from a new perspective prompted me to explore where to go next.

There were choices to be made.

NAFTA

"El respeto al derecho ajeno
Es la paz"

— **Benito Juarez,** National Hero
and President of Mexico (1806 - 1872)

"Among individuals as among nations,
The respect to other people's right is peace"

The U.S./Mexico border is a scar that continues to bleed and I was determined to become a healing agent.

The early 1990's were turning points for Mexico and its role in the world market. Mexico had experienced political turmoil for decades and was transforming itself towards economic growth and stability. It was suffering from the growing pains that NAFTA created, but every crisis brings reno-

Lucía with President Bush and Hispanic leaders at the White House

THE WHITE HOUSE

WASHINGTON

June 7, 1991

Dear Ms. Garcia:

Please accept my heartfelt thanks for your hard work and dedication in helping to assure the extension of fast-track procedures for implementing trade agreements.

As you well know, at issue in the Congressional vote on fast track was whether the United States would maintain its leadership role in the world economy. At stake was our ability to continue to reap the prosperity and jobs that expanded trade has meant and will mean for the United States economy.

Now, thanks to your efforts, we can resume our seat at the bargaining table in the Uruguay Round of multilateral trade talks. We can begin work on a North American Free Trade Agreement. Both negotiations hold enormous promise for the United States, for our neighbors, and for the world trading system.

I look forward to your continued support and counsel as we pursue the negotiation and implementation of trade agreements that are vital to our economic growth.

Best wishes.

Sincerely,

George Bush

Ms. Lucia Garcia
Elan International

Irvine, California 92714

vation. Mexico was going through debt restructuring and developing a social vertebrate. With the knowledge of the Mexican culture, its customs and practices, and political conditions, Élan International became instrumental in helping Mexican companies work on projects involving technology transfer.

I struggled to build a client list and cultivated political allies by working on election campaigns for congressional representatives, U.S. senators, governors, and U.S. presidents. My hard work paid off in the early 1990's. I was asked to join a small group of Latino Business leaders to meet with President Bush and lobby for the ratification of the North America Free Trade Agreement, (NAFTA).

NAFTA opened trade among Canada, the United States, and Mexico, marking a historic milestone with countries south of the border. This is the largest free trade area with more than 400 million people and a gross domestic product or GDP of over US $11.4 trillion according to the Trade and Economic Analysis Division (EET) of the Department of Foreign Affairs and International Trade. With the rest of the Americas joining in, it became the largest trading block in the world.

With the passing of NAFTA, Hispanics were the natural and vital component in making this trade pact a reality. Latinos tend to use their culture and language as a vital element when negotiating with their counterparts in Latin America.

There are more than 200 million people living in poverty in Latin America. My mission was to advance economic integration that would improve the conditions in their regions and create opportunities for them in business and technology transfer. Thus, the people of these nations would find work in their own country and would not have to leave their families behind and emigrate to the U.S.

During the Free Trade Agreement discussions, I received several invitations to visit privileged places such as the White House and Mexico's counterpart, *Los Pinos,* to meet with the respective presidents and other important political figures and collaborate with the process of the treaty. In the global business arena, it is what you know and whom you know that really matters.

Élan International organized the first California-Mexico Business Development Conference to bring together business leaders from both sides of the border. NAFTA was still going through a period of adjustment and it became a test against all odds.

Many challenges occurred during the preparation of the conference; volunteers and staff who were collaborating with this event had a hidden agenda. While I was in Mexico promoting the conference, they took all the information we had gathered for a decade, leaving me alone to finalize the details. I never felt defeated by this situation. People wanting to do business with the two countries poured in, the matchmaking opportunities were unique, and the success in closing deals was a success for Élan International.

By attending seminars, conferences, and conventions in Mexico and the U.S., I received valuable information on global issues and became an important source on NAFTA nationwide. I was interviewed by TV and print media and was invited to lecture on international business practices throughout the U.S. and abroad thus opening doors of opportunity to other businesses and maintaining the United States" leadership role in the world economy.

Mesoamerica: Central and South America – The Andean Condor Meets the American Eagle

South America's majestic condor and the mighty eagle of North America symbolized what was known as Mesoamerica. One of the planet's six cradles of early civilizations was an area occupied by a multiplicity of ancient cultures that shared religious beliefs, art, architecture, and technology, making them unique in our hemisphere for three thousand years.

The U.S./Latin American relationship is of great importance. The U.S. is the Promised Land in the political, business, educational, religious, and cultural arenas. Among all ethnic groups, the U.S./Hispanic market represents the largest ethnic segment in the country and ranks highest among the fastest-growing populations. Immigration has fueled most of the growth in the market. However, the native-born second generation segment of the population will increasingly stimulate a greater proportion of the future growth in the U.S.

According to the 2000 U.S. Census Bureau Population Division, there are 35,305,818 Hispanics representing a $700 billion dollar U.S. Hispanic market. They symbolize an important economic force in the United States.

Hispanic entrepreneurs own more small businesses than any other ethnic group in America. They are influencing mainstream America, their contributions and achievements are enormous, and this cannot be ignored.

Hispanics are poor and wealthy, multi-millionaires, professionals, blue collar, and white-collar workers, Catholics and Jews, Independents, Republicans, and Democrats, white and black, yellow and brown. Multicultural, multiethnic, and multilingual people make up this vast Hispanic population. Many are U.S. citizens and most of the second and third generation have assimilated into American society while maintaining a strong connection to their roots and traditions.

Latinos want a healthy and prosperous America with opportunities to work and to provide their families with the basic needs: health, food, shelter, and a good education.

They also want to participate in community building and in the political process.

I continue to promote investments and exchange technologies to empower the people of these emerging countries. I encourage the business community's involvement to seek solutions, to meet the challenges facing Latin America and to take advantage of the vast opportunities that exist in the United States.

Fortunately, the *Latinization* of the United States of America is happening simultaneous to the *Americanization* of

Latin America, creating economic growth and helping to bridge the differences that have existed.

CHAPTER 9

World Leaders

La construcción de la Paz
Es un proceso que jamás termina...
No podemos ignorar nuestras diferencias
O pasar por alto nuestros intereses comunes.
Se requiere que trabajemos y vivamos unidos.

— **Oscar Arias Sánchez,** Nobel Peace Prize Laureate 1987

Peace is a never-ending process...
It cannot ignore our differences
Nor overlook our common goals.
It compels us to work and live together.

There are times when people and places leave an indelible mark on your passage through life. The probability that you will meet world leaders and share your world vision with them is unlikely. I feel blessed that I have met person-

Lucía with Dr. Oscar Arias Sánchez in his home in Costa Rica

ally with some exceptional individuals across the world. I believe that nothing in life happens by coincidence, and I am guided by my faith and my determination to build bridges of understanding amongst people from all nations.

Dr. Oscar Arias Sánchez

Dr. Oscar Arias Sánchez, President of Costa Rica from 1986-90, then re-elected in 2006, Peacemaker and Leader Among Nations, was the recipient of the Nobel Peace Prize in 1987 for his work to bring peace to Central America.

During his candidacy in 1986, Dr. Arias Sánchez and his then wife Doña Margarita visited Southern California to meet with Costa Rican expatriates living in the United States. I was asked to promote several protocol and fund-raising activities on Dr. Arias Sánchez's behalf. On frequent opportunities, I accompanied him and heard his message about his vision of Peace and Unity in Central America.

It was the beginning of his quest towards the peace-making process he submitted to five Presidents in that region, a process that led to the peaceful solution of a very difficult problem.

His monetary award from the Nobel Peace prize was used to establish the Arias Foundation for Peace and Human Progress with projects to promote equal opportunity for women in all sectors of Central American society, to foster change-oriented philanthropy in Latin America, and work for demilitarization and conflict resolution in developing nations.

In 1989 while I was serving as a Trustee of National University, its president, Dr. Jerry Lee, encouraged me to attend the graduation ceremony at our campus in San José, Costa Rica. My background in Latin American studies was an asset and I used it in all the planned activities. Dr. Arias

Sánchez was present at the ceremony and invited us to join him and his wife at his home in the town of Heredia, his place of birth. We discussed, among other issues, our mutual interest in Simon Bolivar, creator of the Plan for the Pan-American Union, and liberator of the Grand Colombia and of course, my dream for peace.

Meeting Dr. Arias inspired me to carry on with my mission in that region and encouraged me to continue working towards our common goal.

Vicente Fox Quezada

Lucía at the State of The World Forum,
Yael Dayan in the background

President Vicente Fox Quezada of Mexico is a creative thinker and a visionary, a renaissance man and a citizen of the world. The State of the World Forum, chaired by

Mikhail Gorbachev, took place in the city of Guanajuato in November 1995. Organized by Fox Quezada, then Governor of the State of Guanajuato, the forum was a great success. More than 2,000 political, corporate, and religious world leaders attended.

I was invited by Fox Quezada to be one of the speakers to discuss and design a plan on "The Role of Women in the 21st Century." This special forum took place in the main auditorium featuring female authors, politicians, activists, and entrepreneurs.

The city, a UNESCO World Heritage Site since 1988, was heavily guarded to protect the visitors who came from every corner of the globe. All of the speakers stayed in the outskirts of the city in historic hotels and haciendas surrounded by gardens and attractive scenery.

The day of my presentation, I felt apprehensive about the responsibility of the role I had to play in this important world event. I got up at 6 o'clock in the morning and walked directly to the grounds of the Ex Hacienda San Gabriel de Barrera. Located across from the Mission Park Plaza, San Gabriel De Barrera is a historic hilltop resort. Built in the 17th century, it has impressive colonial architecture with pavilions, pools, fountains, and footpaths.

There are seventeen different gardens, each one with its own style and name. I found a little spot hidden from the rest of the landscape. This one was called *El Jardín Rincón de Beatriz,* or Beatriz's Alcove, which owes its name to a charming legend. On its wall was a poetic inscription in colorful mosaic tiles that read as follows:

Oasis de Paz,
Ambiente de Reposo
Que al Cuerpo dá Solaz,
Y al Alma Gozo.

Oasis of Peace,
Most tranquil landscape
That to the body solace gives,
And to the soul delight.

I was later to share this poetic sentiment with the audience at the beginning of my speech, and add, "This epitomizes the Woman."

I continued walking on every path that would lead me into meditation, each a place of prayer where I could contemplate and reflect upon what message I would give to the world. Reminiscing on my early years when my mother took us to the beautiful gardens of the cemetery in my hometown or to visit mausoleums and monuments of historic poets, authors, and presidents, I received my inspiration.

Suddenly, I stopped at the foot of the brick steps that led uphill to a grotto where a statue of the Virgin of Guadalupe, the venerable image of the Mexican people, was positioned. Just before I could reach the top, I came upon a high-ranking Irish Catholic priest who was speaking with one of the faithful and blocking the entrance. I stopped before them and for a few minutes that seemed like an eternity, I waited and waited for them to clear the path. The priest then turned toward me and muttered,

"Not now, my child, not now; I am busy."

"No, Father! It is not you I came to see; it is the Virgin

Mary I wish to visit!" I humbly responded pointing toward the revered figure and bypassing this formal and solemn man.

I appealed to the Virgin of Guadalupe, the Dark Virgin of Latin America, Patroness of Mexico, for strength and asked for her blessings. I wanted to make my presentation with the words that would be equal to this enormous task. Getting closer to the altar, I offered her a bouquet of Lilies of the Valley that I had picked from one of the plots, kneeled at her feet, and respectfully asked her for guidance.

"Virgencita, que quereis que le diga al mundo?"

(Holy Mother, what is the message you would like me to give to the world?)

For a moment I perceived a sound coming from la guadalupana as if she were speaking to me. An almost imperceptible whisper filled the air and my entire body was enveloped in the morning mist. She lifted my spirit and strengthened my resolve to fulfill my mission.

The group was comprised of women who have made a difference in the world. Among them, Isabel Allende, Vice President of the Democratic Party in Chile and daughter of former Chilean President Fernando Allende; Yael Dayan, writer and journalist, member of Parliament of Israel, and daughter of Moshe Dayan – the Israel military commander and statesman. Also Khadija Haq, President of Mahbub ul Haq Human Development Centre of Pakistan; Amalia García, member of the Mexican congress (today Governor of the State of Zacatecas and the first woman governor in Mexico); and Jihan Sadat, political and social activist and widow of President Anwar al-Sadat, of Egypt… and me!

While we waited in the green room, they talked about the significant contributions their parents or husbands had made to the world. I was quiet – unusual for me when I am with a group of people. Then I asked myself,

"What am I doing here with all these renowned leaders, and what contributions had my parents made?"

I recalled that in my family there was a former President of Colombia, Carlos E. Restrepo, and I might have inherited his leadership skill, but who would care now?

With self-confidence, and with flowers from the Virgin of Guadalupe in my hand, I approached the podium. Addressing Governor Vicente Fox Quezada, I said,

"Mr. President, I thank you for your vision in bringing all the world leaders to our hemisphere."

"Mr. President?" The audience responded with exclamations, boos, and applause. This happened four years before his successful bid for the presidency of Mexico. It must have been a premonition based on a woman's intuition or sixth sense.

I spoke about my personal struggles since childhood, the challenges as a Latina immigrant in the United States, the woman's role in a man's world of international business, and the responsibilities of home and community.

I addressed the dilemma at the US-Mexico border and how I was collaborating to make things better, determined to be a healing agent. "Women are *Sacerdotisas de la Paz* (Priestess of Peace) whose mission is to nurture and spread compassion and understanding. There is a universal need to unify men and women and encourage each other to walk together, hand in hand and build a better world," I said.

At the end of my presentation, Governor Fox Quezada came up to the stage and putting his arm around me said, *"Me arrancaste lagrimas del alma"* (you pulled tears out of my soul).

Asia: The Tigers of the Far East – *Marco Polo no Está Solo*

With my participation in the promotion of NAFTA came several invitations from Asia. Traveling to bustling cities, stopovers in small towns in remote areas, visiting factories deep in the treacherous jungle, flying in small planes and helicopters over dangerous mountain peaks, offered an amalgam of opportunities to expand connectivity between businesses and cultures in the Far East. I decided to continue on my journey to other continents and follow Marco Polo's footsteps.

"The finest island of its size in the entire world" said Marco Polo about Sri Lanka, the Teardrop of India, (Ceylon). I traveled there to meet with government officials and entrepreneurs and learn about the prospects this small island offered in trade relations between Asian and Latin American nations.

Lucía with Minister Gamini Dissanayake and officials at his home in Sri Lanka

Despite the warnings of a few well-intentioned associates that I should cancel my trip because of the civil and political friction between the Sinhalese and Tamils, I went ahead with my plans to undertake this adventure.

Sri Lanka is a multi-ethnic, multi-religious country with a diverse and rich culture and a population of 19 million. Almost all of the major religions: Buddhism, Hinduism, Christianity, and Islam are widely worshiped.

On October 24, 1993 on my visit to the island, I was invited to meet with Gamini Dissanayake at his home. He was an outstanding political leader, Social Development Minister, and presidential candidate. He praised my enthusiasm for life, eagerness to learn about other cultures and most of all, my overwhelming zest for life. Looking directly into my eyes he said,

"There are five elements that make a human being: The soul, air, earth, water and fire."

He stopped for an instant and continued,

"And some contain more fire than others."

I responded assuming he was complementing me on my ardor,

"Well I am glad you noticed it."

Then he became rather solemn and said,

"My dear Lucía, we must control that fire and achieve balance among those five elements."

I still remember his advice and constantly make an effort to maintain a sense of balance. He then stated,

"The world begins here and ends here; this is the last human civilization before the South Pole," referring to the two thousand year-old culture of Sri Lanka.

Minister Dissanayake and I prayed for unity and peace in the world. For my protection he presented me with a gold pendant with nine precious gems in the form of a triangle representing the nine planets. We shared books we had both read, ancient wisdom, the politics of U.S. and Mexico and discussed building bridges between the United Sates, Mexico, and Sri Lanka. Teasingly he said to me,

"If you had been born here, you would be prime minister of this country.

Mr. Dissanayake gave me three books, *Fifty: A Beginning* written by him and dedicated to Luis Donaldo Colosio, Secretary of Social Works and presidential candidate of Mexico; one for Senator Dole, the U.S. Republican Leader who was also a candidate for President; and one for me. I promised him that I would deliver them personally, which I did.

One year from the day of our meeting, on October 24, 1994 at fifty-one years of age, Dissanayake along with fifty-eight other people was assassinated by a female suicide bomber believed to be from the Liberation Tigers of Tamil Eemal at a political meeting in the outskirts of Colombo. Coincidentally, Luis Donaldo Colosio was also killed on March 23, 1994 in Tijuana, Mexico. He was only forty-four years old. And Senator Dole lost his bid for the US Presidency that same year.

These events broke my heart but never discouraged me. These world leaders and peacemakers had left me with a legacy which they had shared with me in the privacy of their own homes and offices. I will never forget their place in history, their endless pursuit of unity and peace.

It is said that you never die; and when you pass on, your body goes back to the earth, your spirit goes to heaven, and your knowledge and words live in the minds of those whose lives you touched.

I live my life knowing that we have opportunities to share our knowledge with those among us and to exercise self-discipline, compassion, and tolerance. It is our responsibility.

CHAPTER 10

The High Price of Success

The Thorn Birds

Long ago, there was a bird to sing
Just once in its life.
From the moment it left its nest,
It searched for a thorn tree.
And it never rested until it found one.
Then it began to sing more sweetly
Than any other creature on the face
Of the earth.
And singing, it impaled its breast
On the longest, sharpest thorn.
But as it was dying,
It rose above its own agony
To out-sing the lark and the nightingale.
The thornbird pays its life for that one song
And the whole world stills to listen
And God, in His heaven smiles.
As its best was bought only
At the cost of great pain.

Tony Robbins and Lucía at Mastery University

Driven to the thorn, with no knowledge
Of the dying to come.
But when we press the thorn to our breast,
We know...
We understand...
And still...we do it.

— **Colleen McCullough,** Australian (1937 -)

El Pájaro Que Cantaba Hasta Morir

Hace mucho tiempo atrás, hubo un pájaro
Que cantaba solo una vez en su vida.
Desde el instante en que abandonó su nido,
Buscó un árbol con largas espinas.
Y nunca descansó hasta que lo encontró.
Entonces comenzó a cantar tan dulcemente
Como ninguna otra criatura en la faz de la tierra.

Y mientras cantaba, enterró su pecho
En la espina más larga y afilada.
Y mientras moría, se encumbró más allá de su propia agonía
Para cantar mejor que la calandria y el ruiseñor.

El pájaro que canta hasta morir
Entrega su vida por una sola canción
Y silencioso el mundo entero lo escucha
Y Dios sonríe en su reino celestial.

Cuando damos lo mejor a cambio de un inmenso dolor.
Nos aproximamos a la espina,
Sin comprender que la muerte se acerca.
Pero cuando nos enterramos la espina en nuestro pecho,
Lo reconocemos......
Lo comprendemos......
Y aun así......lo ejecutamos.

In 1994 on Élan's 10th anniversary, we were featured in *Hispanic Business Magazine. Hispanic Business Magazine* was founded in 1979 by Jesus Chavarria, a dynamic *Bridge Builder* between Corporate America and Hispanic America. It is considered the nation's preeminent Hispanic multimedia company. It recognizes the drive, innovation, courage, and civic responsibility of America's most successful Hispanic Entrepreneurs.

My background in international affairs, my dedication to the creation of jobs and the improvement of the living conditions of the less privileged from the developing countries caught the attention of many. The vision of America as a unity motivated me to invest all my efforts into making NAFTA a reality because I saw Mexico as a springboard to the rest of the hemisphere.

I believe that appreciation and respect of other cultures and languages are the perfect ingredients for international communication, so helping corporations achieve a better understanding of the Latin American market became one of my priorities. While working to create a better world, I was brought into a project to build affordable homes on the US-Mexican border.

At the pinnacle of my professional career, several TV, radio, and print media featured my story and my participation in trade pact matters. In 1995, Anthony Robbins watched a segment on NBC-TV where I was discussing the immense opportunities that trade pacts would generate in our hemisphere. Robbins, an American motivational speaker and author, a cultural icon and recognized authority on peak performance, invited me along with a select group of international leaders to speak at one of his powerful conferences called "Mastery University" in Scottsdale, Arizona. I was among the list of world leaders such as spiritual teacher and author Deepak Chopra, American hero Army General Norman Schwarzkopf, Colin Powell, then Chairman of the Joint Chiefs of Staff, and others.

My speech *"Building Bridges: In Search of the Americas Dream"* was unfamiliar to many, and in addition, my name was not recognized among the world's influential.

My performance that evening marked the transcendental moment of my existence. Addressing a crowd of over 2,500 people from sixty-two countries, I entered the stage with the celebrated Andean song *"El Condor Pasa."* The music filled the air and the anticipation was evident. By now the audience must be thinking, "Who is Lucía De García, and what is she doing here?"

Nevertheless, my message received an overwhelmingly positive response. The audience identified with every word I said:

"I am an immigrant, a daughter, a mother, a wife, a friend, and a business owner, and I overcame every stereotype and adversity to achieve success."

During my speech, I described people I had met and places I had visited across the Americas, filling my personal stories with metaphors, my spiritual beliefs, and my vision and mission in life.

Upon conclusion, I presented Tony with three purple orchids, the official flower of Colombia.

"These orchids represent beauty and the color purple represents spirituality," I added.

My gift to Tony was symbolic, asking him to uplift the rest of the continent with the force and eloquence of his motivational message. Upon his gracious acceptance of this challenge, once more was the room filled with the another magical song from the Andes, "Pampa Lirima."

My parting sentiment to those assembled was,

"I invite you all to visit the rest of the Americas, to bring your dreams and hopes, your hearts, your compassion, and your knowledge; let us move beyond the borders, both material and spiritual, both real and imagined, that divide us, and let us fulfill the vision of one united America. If we do, I promise you that we will find that proverbial, and for me, metaphorical pot of gold at the end of the rainbow, measured not only in material wealth, but in brotherhood, tolerance, mutual respect and understanding."

As these feelings invaded my very heart and soul, I had never in my life experienced so much emotion- I felt the force of an epiphany. The tears that followed were not mine alone. I could see them on the faces of many in the audience who at that moment understood that they too could overcome life's ever-present hardships and tribulations.

"What is her power?" asked Tony Robbins as I exited the stage.

"Love" the audience responded.

Tony continued, "Love is her power and with resolve she has been able to accomplish the impossible. What an insight to see countries and people alike..."

As I came off the stage, the crowd was waiting for me outside. Clinging to every word I uttered, they expected me to answer every question they had about life. Overwhelmed and exhausted, I walked back to my hotel room, at times leaning against the wall for support and barely closing my eyes. Suddenly, from behind me, I heard a voice whisper, "You need help," but I could not look back. I tried to listen and sensed this was a message from above; someone was watching over me, warning me.

I entered my hotel room and felt nauseated; my head was bursting, I was short of breath, and had chest pains. I threw myself on the bed and tried to reach the phone to communicate to my family about the profound emotions I had experienced while addressing this crowd.

I don't know who called the paramedics. They arrived by midnight and carefully examined me. I insisted that I was fine and refused to get on the stretcher. Then they asked me to sign a release that would free them of any responsibility in case I didn't go with them and anything went wrong. I signed it and was rushed to the nearest hospital in Tempe. In the emergency room, I could hear the commotion when they diagnosed me and discovered that I had had a near-fatal heart attack or MI, a catastrophic event. Myocardial infarction (MI) is the irreversible necrosis of heart muscle probably caused by an intense emotion. This usually results from an imbalance of oxygen supply and demand. Approximately 1.5 million Americans have acute MI annually, of which 500,000 die. Within a year of MI, 25% of men and 38% of women die.

At three o'clock in the morning, my husband Álvaro received a phone call in California. Lucía Carolina was on a business trip in Atlanta, and Claudia María, was staying with friends. The hospital staff informed them that I might not make it through the night, so they arrived the next morning anxious and fearful of what we all thought would be our last "good-byes."

"Why me?" I was not a candidate for a heart attack. I always took care of myself.

Women like me are supposed to be invincible.

"What if I die? God, I am not yet ready to die. I have not fulfilled my mission on earth. It isn't fair!"

I felt exhausted, drained, and considered giving up at that moment.

I was a prisoner of my own culture. Working seventeen hours a day, trying to be everything to everybody, making sacrifices, and becoming a superwoman, determined to prove to my relatives back in Colombia and to my immediate family that I could succeed in the face of adversity.

The next day doctors performed a catheterization; an extra aortic balloon was used to temporarily stabilize me. I was extremely lucky that there was no rupture of the artery.

Flower arrangements filled the room, among them, a huge one from Tony Robbins with 120 small Hawaiian orchids, perhaps to remind me that what we give comes back a hundredfold.

Álvaro and the girls stayed at a nearby hotel and came to the hospital every day. Phone calls from abroad poured in, one in particular from my brother Iván Darío from Colombia who asked me to connect with the Universe and bring the beams of light of different colors to my heart.

What was he talking about?

I did not understand a word he was saying. However, I followed his instructions and soon I started to heal.

After twelve days in intensive care, taking special medications to stabilize my blood flow, and getting instructions on how to balance my eating habits and reduce stress, the doctors allowed me to fly home. A sense of fear was my turning point. The moment of my recovery became a time of discovery. I learned to pace myself and to love the one that mattered most at that moment: me.

A month later, my brother Iván Darío came to California and we spent days walking on the beach, talking about our childhood and all those years I had missed seeing my siblings grow up while I was away. He coached me on meditation and showed me how to see the world beyond myself and to make peace with myself.

Part III

BRIDGES FOR UNITY AND PEACE

Peace Makers

The bird is traditionally associated
With peace and serenity.
This three-dimensional Bird by Botero
Also signifies the joy of living
And the power of optimism.

The UOB believes that so long
As there is peace and optimism
Among its people, Singapore
Will continue to grow and prosper.

Botero's sculpture allows
One the pleasure of caressing reality.
There is a sensual complicity
That the artist has with his creation
Which is shared with the public.

INSCRIPTION AT THE BASE
OF THE BOTERO SCULPTURE

El pájaro por tradición representa
La paz y la serenidad.
Este Pájaro en tres dimensiones
Creado por Botero

Fernando Botero
Colombian artist,
1932 –
Bronze EA I/2 – 245
x 310 x 250 CM
1990

Walking on the UOB Plaza along the Singapore River, I marveled at the remarkable art around this area and captured this Botero sculpture. (In the background is the Cavenagh Bridge.)

También simboliza el placer de sentirse vivo
Y el poder de la esperanza.

United Overseas Bank (UOB) tiene
La certeza que mientras exista la paz
Y la confianza entre su gente,
Singapore continuará creciendo y progresando.

La escultura de Botero nos permite
Uno de los placeres de contemplar la realidad.
Existe una confabulación sensual
Entre el artista y su creación
La cual es compartida con su publico.

A Pilgrimage for Unity and Peace

Dr. Jane Goodall and Lucía at Jane's Peak in Gombe, Tanzania

Jane Goodall, United Nations Messenger of Peace

Every individual matters.
Every individual has a role to play.
Every individual makes a difference.
And we have a choice:
What sort of difference do we want to make?

Cada individuo es importante.
Cada individuo tiene un destino.
Cada individuo marca la diferencia.
Y todos tenemos una alternativa:
¿Qué clase de diferencia queremos marcar?

— Dr. Jane Goodall

How did I meet Dr. Jane Goodall?

This is a question I am frequently asked. My work with the Multicultural Institute for Leadership (MIL), which I founded in 1995, reached many institutions throughout the world. I always keep in touch with people who cross my path and they remain a source of information for my community projects.

My friend, Jonathan Hutson, then Executive Director of the Western Justice Center in Pasadena conducted diversity and peace dialogues for the MIL and for the Colombian government peace process. He submitted my name to the Jane Goodall Institute (JGI) Board of Trustees for consideration.

Founded by Dr. Goodall in 1977, JGI is a leading international organization that focuses on wildlife research programs, education, advocacy, and undertakes conservation projects and community development. A renowned British ethologist and authority on wild chimpanzees, Dr. Goodall studied under the guidance of the legendary Dr. Louis Leakey in the '60s. Her legacy of over 40 years of pioneering chimpanzee research and advocacy is the longest running project of its kind in the world.

In 2002, Dr. Goodall visited Southern California and decided we should meet face to face. I arranged a private luncheon at the prestigious Center Club in Costa Mesa with community leaders. For the first time in my life, I heard her lecture on the environment, animal conservation, and children's education issues. She amazed me with her message. Her presence filled the room and I was mesmerized by her words – especially with the significance of her mission as a United Nations "Messenger of Peace" and her impact on the minds of millions across the world.

After she had autographed her book *A Reason for Hope,* we both moved into a private area of the club and conversed for more than two hours about mutual concerns, especially about the threat of war between the United States and Iraq. We talked about people we have met, places we have been, and our vision for the planet. Her mission and vision resonated with my mother's – a combination of science and the spirit.

At four o'clock that afternoon, I arrived home and practically collapsed on my bed. There had been times when I had doubted my efforts and asked myself:

What is happening in my life?

What am I doing here in this world?

What is my mission?

Moved by Dr. Goodall's dedication to heal the world, I felt both emotionally exhausted and spiritually renewed. I went to sleep for a couple of hours and when I opened my eyes, I started to cry.

I felt a sense of happiness and a sense of responsibility descend upon me.

I saw Dr. Goodall the next morning and shared my feelings with her. "When you have tears in your eyes, there is a rainbow in your heart," she said quoting an ancient wisdom. I realized that even though I had worked for years on behalf of the community on different levels, I had not been engaged in environmental issues.

At that moment I became dedicated to her cause. Her projects touched me deeply. JGI's program Roots n' Shoots with 6,000 groups in 95 countries nurtures a young generation to bring positive change that inspires action.

Dr. Goodall changed my life by broadening my vision. I now work on humanitarian causes as part of my message for peace throughout the world. She invited me to become a member of the Board of Trustees of the JGI, which has allowed me the privilege to participate in her research projects, gain knowledge by visiting these magnificent places on earth, and demonstrate the power of individual action to change the world. I have found the perfect vehicle to continue my mission to build understanding across boundaries in my quest for Unity and Peace.

A Journey to Africa

In the summer of 2004, several JGI trustees met in Dar Es Salaam, Tanzania, the birthplace of the Jane Goodall Institute's Roots & Shoots program. Swahili is the official tongue and with some knowledge of basic expressions of the language, I was ready to make an effort at cross-cultural communication. It was my first visit to this part of the

African continent, and I was to make in-depth discoveries, to gain a wealth of knowledge of astonishing cultures, of people, landscapes, of rich African traditions, of this mysterious and alluring region.

We flew to Kigoma where Dr. Goodall was waiting for us. This town is the base of the community conservation project, TACARE. We visited the villages of Mkongoro and its infrastructure, Kalinzi, the Kisozi demonstration plot, Mkigo, the dispensary and the protected water spring, Nyarubanda, the forestry demonstration plot, and Ujiji Hybridization. I was astonished by the results of these magnificent projects.

We traveled by boat to the Stream Research Center at Gombe National Park on the coast of Lake Tanganyika. For hours we explored the depths of these mysterious mountains; we hiked through fertile forests and admired the colorful wildlife. Here we discovered the untamed wilderness and observed the amazing world of the chimpanzee, baboon, and monkey in their habitat.

Gombe National Park is a sacred place for Dr. Goodall. When she arrived on the shores of Lake Tanganyika in 1960 as a young woman, it was the fulfillment of her childhood dream.

My dream had been to someday visit this mountain. Dr. Goodall stills visits Jane's Peak where she observes chimpanzees and where research programs are being conducted.

After hours of steep climbing through thorny brush in scorching heat with the assistance of some of my fellow trekkers, I finally reached the top. Dr. Goodall was already at the peak anxiously waiting for all of us, especially for me; she sensed beforehand that I had some physical ailments and wasn't sure I would make it.

When I finally arrived, she and I sat quietly for a few minutes at the same location where she had studied chimpanzees for decades. I could sense her sadness about how much this place had changed. We contemplated the vast mountain and the fires and the deforestation effects that had damaged this treasured land. I prayed for strength and whispered to her,

"I know our mothers are watching us from heaven."

Tears ran slowly down my face and an extraordinary sensation filled my heart. The wind and a sense of peace pleasantly caressed my body and soul. In this place, I perceived the sound of silence; that moment in space and time became one of the highlights of my existence. I had experienced the spiritual and the wild, the luxurious and the soulful.

On our way down we stopped at the waterfalls, a revered space where chimpanzees bathe in the late afternoon. I chose a special place and sat quietly contemplating this moment.

Then what we were waiting for happened – the rare opportunity to observe chimpanzees in their habitat. As we approached them, we stood a few feet from their playground and silently watched them. Sitting under the tree was a family of seven. We observed how they playfully touched and nurtured each other, ignoring our presence.

With some of the locals and the staff of TACARE who accompanied us on this trip, we exchanged candid ideas about cultural interactions and about the differences between men and women, wealth and poverty between the two continents, Africa and America.

Then we flew on a small eight-seat plane to Nanyuki, Kenya to go on a safari. Nearby, on the outskirts of this town, there is the 24,000-acre Sweetwaters Game Reserve. We camped in a deluxe-tented site and had our meals in front of a water hole where magnificent creatures gather during the day.

At night, we cruised on legendary plains in a four-wheel drive vehicle as driver guides illuminated the deepest darkness with their floodlights while tracking wild animals: lions, rhinos, buffaloes, and leopards. A herd of elephants approached us and we quietly waited for several minutes, watching them retreat with their offspring behind them.

We visited the 200-acre Jane Goodall Institute Chimpanzee Sanctuary where abused chimps are rehabilitated and are taught to fend for themselves. As we played with two orphaned baby chimps born in captivity, broken-heartedly I wondered how we could stop this tragic chimp trade.

Next, we took a flight to the bustling center of Nairobi. Driving through the Kenyan countryside in the Ngong Hills with its rural serenity and beauty, I caught sight of the spectacular coffee farm once owned by Danish writer Karen von Blixen (a.k.a. Isak Dinesen) author of *Out of Africa* who said:

"God made the world round so we could never be able to see too far down the road."

Countless times have I had the good fortune to be with Dr. Goodall, whether at board meetings, discussions of future projects in Latin America, fund raisers at private homes, or on cruises to watch the dolphins, and to celebrate life. She is joy, she is peace, she is strength and determination; she is an unending source of hope and inspiration to everyone whose life she touches.

We have prayed together for those who have departed and for those who have hope for the world. Dr. Goodall travels tirelessly for more than 300 days of the year on her quest to make a better world. She is a genuine "Bridge Builder" and a Messenger for Unity and Peace.

Nelson Mandela, Nobel Peace Prize 1993

I have fought against white domination,
And I have fought against black domination.
I have cherished the ideal of a democratic and
Free society in which all persons live together
In harmony and with equal opportunities.
It is an ideal, which I hope to live for
And to achieve. But if needs be, it is an ideal
For which I am prepared to die.

— **Nelson Mandela,** 1993 Nobel Peace Prize in the Rivonia Trial,
Pretoria Supreme Court, 20 April 1964

He luchado contra la dominación de la raza blanca,
Y he luchado contra la dominación
de la raza negra.
He respetado el ideal de una sociedad democrática
Y libre en la que todas las personas
Viven juntas en armonía y compartiendo
Las mismas oportunidades.
Es mi ideal, el cual espero sobrevivir
Y poder alcanzar. Pero si es necesario,
Es un ideal por el cual estoy preparado a morir.

Africa, The Cradle of Humankind.

The ancient archeology at the Cradle of Humankind in South Africa was particularly significant to explore and prepared me for my visit to East Africa with Dr. Jane Goodall.

A memorable experience was my visit in 2004 to the entertainment and corporate capital of the African continent, Johannesburg, a dynamic, vibrant, and cosmopolitan city.

This region has gone through a political transformation and a profound socio-economic change.

Nelson Mandela's life symbolizes the triumph of the human spirit over man's inhumanity to man. His work personifies struggle on behalf of South Africans who suffered and sacrificed so much to bring peace to their land. He accepted the Nobel Peace Prize as an accolade to all people who have worked for peace and stood against racism.

In May 2004, the Sandton Square was renamed the Nelson Rolihlahla Mandela Square in commemoration of ten years of democracy in South Africa. In the past it had been perceived as the preeminent symbol of commercial and social elitism and was one of the largest public open spaces in South Africa.

I was there during the festivities marking the unveiling of the world's first public statue of Nelson Mandela, the man who led his country across the apartheid divide and who throughout his life has championed the cause of the oppressed and disadvantaged. To stand beside this larger-than-life, six-meter tall bronze statue was quite an experience and it will be a constant reminder of Nelson Mandela's courageous life long struggle to eliminate apartheid and a tribute to the spirit of the people of South Africa.

The Dalai Lama

The Dalai Lama at California State

Today, more than ever before,
life must be characterized by a sense
of Universal responsibility,
not only nation to nation and human to human,
but also human to other forms of life.

— ***The Dalai Lama,*** Tibet (1935 -)

Hoy, más que nunca,
debemos llevar la vida con un sentido
de responsabilidad universal,
no solamente de nación a nación
y de persona a persona,
sino también en relación a otras formas de vida.

In 2000, I joined the Center for Religious Studies in America at California State University, Fullerton (CSUF). Dr. Benjamin Hubbard, a professor of comparative religion and an expert in faith-based initiatives directed this program. Participating in the discussions was Ambassador Ananda Guruge, a devout Buddhist born in Sri Lanka and a supreme authority on the world's major religions. I was profoundly inspired by his integrity, his generous heart and his life of simplicity.

Others religious leaders represented every denomination on earth. My role was to create bridges of understanding between the business community and the respective varieties of philosophy and religion.

His Holiness, the 14th Dalai Lama, a spiritual leader, considered the manifestation of Avalokiteshvara (the Lord of Compassion) whose role is to rescue others from suffering, had fled from Tibet along with his followers when China invaded his beloved Tibet, and he has been in exile ever since then. The dedication with which he has pursued global human rights won him the Nobel Peace Prize in 1989.

When the Dali Lama visited CSUF in June 2000, I joined President Milton A. Gordon and other executives and religious representatives of Cal State Fullerton to take part in a ceremony to plant a Bodhi tree.

It was a bright sunny day as the Dalai Lama ceremoniously blessed the Bodhi tree in the subtropical garden of the Fullerton Arboretum. Dr. Ben Hubbard – Jewish, Robert McLaren – Christian, Radha Bhattacharya – Hindu, and Nawang Phuntsog – Buddhist, each representing his religious faith, lifted a golden shovel to fill in soil around the tree in front of a crowd of spectators.

According to tradition, Siddhartha, the founder of Buddhism, sat under a bodhi tree when he became enlightened some 2,500 years ago. The tree, whose Latin name is *Ficus religiosa,* can grow up to 100-feet high, 200 feet wide and live to be 2,000 years.

At the Becker Amphitheater, with hundreds of attendees, His Holiness spoke to us in a soft voice and entertained us with anecdotes that were both spiritually elevating and humorous, blessed the audience, and placed scarves on people's shoulders.

The Dalai Lama's visit made an impact on me and on those who attended the ceremony. Occasionally I go to the Arboretum to meditate at the foot of this tree, which is a permanent remembrance of this event. These experiences contributed immensely to my spiritual development and magnified both my understanding and appreciation of the world's many religions.

A Pilgrimage for Unity and Peace

Lucía with Father Anthony Delisi, OCSO, at the Holy Spirit Monastery

Everyone carries deep inside a loving bell.
That bell is called the heart.
This heart resonates,
and is my desire that yours
play precious melodies.

— **Pope John Paul II** (1978 - 2005)

Cada uno de nosotros lleva en sí (dentro)
una campana muy sensible.
Esa campana se llama corazón.
Este corazón suena,
y es mi augurio que el vuestro
interprete siempre bellas melodías.

My pilgrimage through life is part of a perpetual walk, one that has led me to remote countries to visit monasteries, convents, Romanesque gothic churches, and Rococo, Baroque and Neo-classic basilicas and cathedrals. I wander through unknown regions, religious paths traveled by Celtics and Romans, saints and warriors.

These historical places, museums, cemeteries, gardens and monuments inspire my respect for all that is sacred and help me build a bridge between the past and the present and unify them with the spirit.

My walk is without pretensions. It is filled with a desire to connect with the hearts of the people I encounter along the way – people of all ages, diverse ethnic backgrounds, and personalities, comprising the full spectrum of the human spirit.

In the spring of 2004, I traveled to Europe to restore my failing health and to rejuvenate my spirit. This pilgrimage had an objective: To take responsibility for my own actions.

Before leaving for Europe, I stopped in Conyers, Georgia -30 miles outside Atlanta. On a hidden and tranquil road stands the Roman Catholic Monastery of Our Lady of the Holy Spirit of the Cistercian Order of the Strict Observance (Trappist). The monks dedicate themselves to the worship of God in a hidden life within the monastery under the Rule of St Benedict.

This is a community totally oriented to a contemplative life of prayer. They lead a monastic way of life in solitude and silence, in constant prayer and blissful atonement. I had heard about Fray Anthony Delisi and had long wanted to meet him. Father Delisi is a venerated monk, an author who has served his community for more than fifty years. I approached the sales clerk behind the desk at the Abbey Store.

"May I see Fray Anthony Delisi?" I asked softly.

"What is your name? Do you have an appointment with him?" she said, annoyed at my boldness.

"I am on a very important mission and I must see him," I responded.

She phoned Father Anthony at his hidden retreat. The Father was curious about this unexpected visit and asked her to direct me to his office. I walked through the pristine gardens and into a corridor to a cloister room where he sat quietly. With a full head of hair, a gray beard, and a smile I will never forget, he struck me as a person who reflected his spirituality in every sense. He asked me what I wanted.

"I am on my way to Rome to have an audience with His Holiness Pope John Paul II." I responded

Father Anthony was rather surprised,

"You must have good contacts."

"Yes I do, God is my contact" I responded by pointing up to the heavens.

With a grin, he proceeded with the protocol. I asked for his blessings and let him know that I had brought requests from relatives and friends who appealed to me as a conduit for their healing.

After praying together and discussing spirituality, I told Father Anthony about my quest for unity and peace between the spiritual and the material world.

He asked for a special favor and handed me an autographed book entitled *"What Makes a Cistercian Monk?"* written by him.

"Can you give this gift to the Holy Father for me?"

"Most certainly" I responded, and left the gardens of the Monastery feeling hopeful and confident.

On to Rome, the Holy place.

I traveled with a group of pilgrims from different regions of the American hemisphere accompanied by two Catholic priests and a spiritual counselor, Flor María, who sustained us in prayer throughout this journey. It was a blessing and an opportunity of a lifetime to have an audience at St. Peter's Square with His Holiness John Paul II ten months before he passed on. By a gift of God or because we arrived earlier, we took seats in the first row in front of the canopy where the Pope sits.

The Holy Father's health was deteriorating and he could barely move. However, his spiritual strength and charisma were remarkable. He made his entrance in the Pope Mobile; suddenly, a light as bright as sunrise struck us, so bright it was almost blinding. Speaking softly, almost in a whisper, the Pope addressed the faithful in different languages:

"I greet the young people, the sick people and the newlyweds, and in this month of May that has just begun, I invite them to renew their devotion to Our Lady."

He was making a tremendous effort to carry on with his mission until the end and to leave us a legacy to continue our efforts to build a world of Unity and Peace.

I held the religious paraphernalia I had brought in front of me to capture his blessings. On my travels across the world, I had made an effort to attend any Mass celebrated by him, whether in Mexico, New York, Colombia, Rome, or Los Angeles.

Being in the presence of His Holiness was enlightening, a joyful moment I will always carry deep in my heart for as long as I live.

Leaving Italy, we traveled by plane and by car to Spain and France and enjoyed the most breathtaking views, unforgettable landscapes, and countryside. Experiencing medieval and Etruscan history along the way, I visited small towns and villages, birthplaces of saints and shrines where the Blessed Mother Mary, the Queen of Heaven has appeared on earth hundreds of times, especially during the most crucial moments in history.

El Camino de Santiago de Compostela is a Patrimony of Humanity of the UNESCO World Heritage Centre and has the power of seduction. The magic of El Camino is found in *"ir despacio,"* (more slowly,) with the support of each person you find along the way.

Pilgrims from all religions and faiths take this journey, walking twelve miles per day, 500 miles in seven weeks seeking spiritual significance to purify their spirit in search of a transcendental transformation and a process of spiritual regeneration. It is a magical bridge between matter and spirit, of history and legends, and of all beliefs and religions.

Near El Camino's path tucked away in the mountains of Santander sits the remote village of San Sebastian de Garabandal. This quiet and peaceful place was once the site of an event that drew thousands of people from all over the world. Since 1961, four young girls – Conchita, Jacinta, Mari Loli, and Mari Cruz have claimed that St. Michael the Archangel announced the apparition of the Virgin Mary. The girls alleged that she had appeared to them dozens of times.

I was a guest at the home of Jacinta's sister, Marcelina, where I had homemade meals of hearty soups and country breads and plenty of story telling with other pilgrims who came from all over the world.

I took a vow of silence for five hours every morning to meditate. Silence is one of the Cistercian observances, "where we are able to quiet the interior to be open and free to experience and be in the presence of the One who made us and loves us," wrote Fray Anthony on his book.

There is a quiet place in the pines, a cluster of trees above the village where many of the apparitions took place. I hiked up the mountain and when I arrived at the top, I lay down on the venerated ground and gazed into the sky and prayed for those who are no longer with us and for those of in need of healing.

Overlooking this magnificent landscape, I realized that the hastily paced life I lived was doing me harm. Inside of me was something larger than life, wanting always to do more than I could handle. My spirit was running faster than my body; I was feeling tired and finally stopped and said,

"Please wait for me."

I had a spiritual experience and recognized the immense power of God in my life. I had a mission to fulfill and it was time for my spiritual rebirth.

Part of my mission is to bond my physical body, mind and soul, to take more time for meditation, and to practice silence; this deepens my understanding of the universe.

The Miracle at Lourdes – the Prayer Capital

There are only two ways to live your life.
One is as though nothing is a miracle.
The other is as if everything is.

— **Albert Einstein** (1879-1955)

Solo hay dos maneras de vivir tu vida.
La una es como si nada fuera milagroso.
La otra es como si todo lo fuera.

Lourdes is hope, Lourdes is healing, and Lourdes is compassion for those who feel abandoned.

Here in 1858 the Blessed Mother of Jesus, the Immaculate Conception, first appeared to a young girl named Bernadette in a small rock grotto. A miraculous freshwater spring believed to have healing powers began flowing at the grotto of Massabielle, also known as the Miraculous Cave and the Cave of Apparitions. Water purifies the soul, and it is the source of life.

A miracle is a sign from God which many have experienced. I was there to pray for a miracle that would heal my body, inspire my heart and bestow inner peace for my soul through the sacred water that flows constantly from the spring at Lourdes.

In this remarkable town, I had a most inspiring experience when I witnessed thousands of ailing pilgrims who had come from all over the world to cleanse their spirits and heal their bodies.

Heavy rain came pouring down. When it rains in Lourdes, it is as if heaven were cleaning our impurities. I went to the nearby bathhouse, a sacred shrine. Rows of people from every corner of the world waited their turn while singing *Alleluia* and *Ave María* in Latin, the universal Christian language. Men and women were separated on each side of the entrance and you could feel the excitement and anticipation of the moment.

Nuns and nurses helped the sick through this experience with tenderness and care and assisted in the transition between the mundane and the spiritual in what seemed a brief moment in time. Behind curtains, I disrobed and the caretakers shielded my body with a white sheet. The asked me if I had any particular request to cure so they could pray along with me.

Completely naked, I slowly immersed myself in the freezing spring waters and was guided toward the other side of the pool where a small white image of the Virgin Mary awaited.

I experienced a miraculous sensation and a spiritual renaissance. When I reached this beloved image, I burst into a mystical weeping and asked the nurses to pour the water over my entire body. I wanted to remain there forever.

A divine intervention occurred; it was sublime, uplifting, moving, and inspiring! A mysterious force was at work in that unknown region between science and faith. It was a testament to the sudden improvement in my health which had been slowly deteriorating that I suddenly felt transformed and became a living witness to a miracle.

On the other side of the grotto, people filled their containers with this blessed water. I poured the holy water into several plastic bottles shaped like the Virgin Mary to bring home to my family and friends who were in need of spiritual, physical, or emotional healing.

These moving religious experiences reinforced my commitment to strengthen the bond between the material and the spiritual world

MIL
MULTICULTURAL
GREECE

CHAPTER 12

My Life Purpose

If

If you can keep your head when all about you
Are losing theirs and blaming it on you;
. . .If you can meet with Triumph and Disaster
And treat those two impostors just the same. . .

If you can talk with crowds
and keep your virtue,
Or walk with Kings –
nor lose the common touch. . .

If you can fill the unforgiving minute
With sixty seconds' worth of distance run,
Yours is the Earth and everything that's in it,
And – which is more – you'll be a Man,
my son.

— **Rudyard Kipling**, Born in Bombay, India (1865 - 1936)

The Multicultural Institute for Leadership Convocation At Angels Anaheim Stadium

Si

***Si** guardas en tu puesto, la cabeza tranquila,*
Cuando todo a tu lado es cabeza perdida.

*. . .**Si** tropiezas el triunfo, si llega tu derrota,*
Y a los dos impostores les tratas de igual forma.
***Si** hablas con el pueblo y guardas tu virtud.*

***Si** marchas junto a reyes con tu paso y tu luz.*

***Si** llenas un minuto envidiable y cierto,*

De sesenta segundos que te lleven al cielo. . . .
Todo lo de esta tierra, será de tu dominio,
Y mucho mas aún, serás hombre, hijo mío.

The excerpts from this poem have inspired me to follow my purpose in life. I trust it will make an impact in your lives as well.

When I was a little girl, the local radio stations occasionally made emergency announcements to all the car owners in the city of Medellin to come to the airport and turn the lights on to light up the landing field. The old airport was one of the most dangerous airports in the world. It was located in the middle of the city surrounded by mountains, so aircraft had great difficulty landing after dark.

Years later, "bring together the lights" became a metaphor when I gathered community leaders to create a multicultural organization to bridge the differences among people of the United State of America.

"This is what we are here for, to bring together the lights – lights bright enough to spread across and illuminate the world," I constantly reminded everyone.

In 2000, I visited my native Colombia to celebrate my high school reunion. One of my schoolmates, a social worker, asked me to go into a remote shantytown called *Santo Domingo Savio,* situated in one of the poorest districts on the outskirts of Medellín. There I saw a community project designed to reintegrate the inhabitants of the region into the social order, provide education, and build new homes.

I was invited to deliver a message of unity and peace to those who live in extreme poverty. As I began to address the crowd, a rather thin and dark-complexioned young man of about fourteen years of age tried to disrupt my presentation by making loud noises in the back of the room.

His name was Duvian. His hand was holding something inside his shirt; I asked him to show me what he was hiding. He pulled out a weapon (I later found out it was fake). I invited him to come forward and sit in the front row. Self-assured, I continued to deliver my speech offering words of hope, of a future full of expectations, and shared with them the difficulty of adapting to another country. I finished my message by saying:

"With perseverance and hard work you too can conquer the seemingly impossible, and like me, become a citizen of the world."

After my presentation, I invited Duvian to sit with me and persuaded him to tell me his story. It was a school day and I was wondering why he did not attend school.

"Nobody wants to associate with me because of my color," he declared.

"Prejudice still exists in this world, even in the most advanced civilizations," I said, but I assured him that there were many people like me fighting every day to do something about it.

His only desire was to own a motorcycle and become a "sicario" or a killer-for-hire. In our lengthy conversation I did all I could to encourage him to pursue other constructive avenues that would lead him toward a much more positive environment, acquire financial freedom, and become a better person.

"With education, you can achieve it," I echoed my mother's advice.

My words were not in vain. A few months later I called the social worker and director in charge of this project and asked about Duvian. Much to my delight, she informed me that he had become a community organizer in charge of about 400 youths and was coordinating groups of leadership.

I phoned him occasionally to monitor his progress.

"Duvian, what made you change?" I asked him.

"When you told us that one person's change can transform 250 people and each one can change another 250, I realized that this is how we can change the world."

What a great satisfaction one feels in knowing the powerful impact words can have on people's lives! A vision of a multicultural democracy and a tapestry of cultures can be achieved by having an open mind and showing tolerance for all.

That is how we all can make a difference.

Multiculturalism – Cultural integration

The American landscape has changed in the last fifty years and to live in a united and peaceful society requires that those who come from diverse cultures be guided by leaders in business, religion, education, and government who understand and respect those differences.

As long as we are intolerant of and obstinate about our differences, of whatever kind, there will be violence. To create a world that appreciates all cultures and create awareness, tolerance, and respect for all people has long been my foremost priority.

In 1995 I created the Multicultural Institute for Leadership (MIL). "Finding commonalities and celebrating differences" is our motto. I saw my mission in life transformed into reality. That mission was to build a collaborative, interdependent, and inclusive society and to help those who have come to this country with hopes and dreams of building new lives in a free society.

The goals set by MIL placed it at the vanguard of immigrants' issues. We created seminars on multiculturalism where we discussed social themes of race, class, sex, ethnicity, or age discrimination in our communities.

These monthly dialogues were attended by leaders of government, business, educational institutions, religious and community-based organizations. MIL shared the experiences and results of these dialogues locally, state and nation-wide, as well as internationally. We were making an impact on our society for the next century and transcending borders, religions, and races by building coalitions.

MIL became a catalyst and a driving force on the subjects of diversity and multiculturalism, determined to influence others.

Our mission coincided with that of various political institutions and corporations such as The International Channel Networks (ICN) which provides in-language and multi-ethnic programming in the United States and in more than twenty Asian, European, and Middle Eastern languages. Corporations have started to hire Diversity Community representatives to bridge the gap between mainstream America and the ethnic consumer.

In my quest for Unity and Peace I have addressed many diverse groups though the years, from the prestigious Syracuse University in New York, the New Horizons, a home for abandoned girls in Utica, NY, to several ethnic Chambers of Commerce. I have discussed the impact of diversity on corporate America and how we can make a difference in the 21st Century. I have also addressed crowds on how Mexico can become "The Springboard to the Rest of Latin America: The Cultural Traits Demystified."

This has been my way of helping to create a world of understanding and an effective way to break through the barriers that exist today among various ethnic groups.

To transform our societies, the infrastructure must be there to support people with vision and to link human beings through understanding, respect and tolerance.

Many Perspectives, One Vision

Most immigrants have assimilated into American society, but there are those few who will never consider themselves *Americans.* Instead, they hold on to their cultural roots and use them as a shield, creating boundaries instead of bridges to other ethnic groups.

As an immigrant to this great nation, as a self-made entrepreneur and owner of an international consulting business, it has been my privilege and honor to collaborate with several international organizations and thus to give back to the community.

I encourage you all to become an inspiration in your society and to count your blessings that you are in this country. At the same time approach your future with passion and with a desire to be productive. Integrate your children into the mainstream while preserving your culture as you adapt to multicultural America.

It is your duty to shape your vision and to individualize your voice through the inclusion of racial, political, historic, geographic, spiritual, social, economic, and cultural dimensions. The goal is to live and work together, side by side, as one unified human race.

I see enormous potential for students from diverse backgrounds to participate in the areas of leadership, innovation, and community service. We come from immigrant families of many experiences and perspectives and come together because we share common values and a common vision.

We arrive in the United States as first, second, or third-generation world citizens from many different lands, cultures, and creeds. Native-born, male and female, we have business interests all over this nation. Therefore, we must all see the importance of mentoring youth to be future leaders of our diverse and wonderful communities.

Envision the possibilities and rewards that come from collaborating, despite our differences, to develop new business models to serve new markets. No less important is our need to unite in a collective desire to work together and to shape a better future for our children and our families.

CHAPTER 13

Everything Is Possible
¡Si Se Puede!

The Eagle & The Wolf

There is a great battle that rages inside me.
One side is the soaring eagle.
Everything the eagle stands for
Is good and true and beautiful,
And it soars above the clouds.
Even though it dips down into the valleys,
It lays its eggs on the mountaintops.
The other side of me is the howling wolf.
And that raging, howling wolf represent
The worst that is in me.
He eats upon my downfalls and
Justifies himself by his presence in the pack.

Who wins this great battle?
The one I feed!

— **Author Unknown**

El Águila y el Lobo

Hay una gran batalla frenética dentro de mí.
A un lado está la encumbrada águila.
Todo lo que el águila simboliza

The Soaring Eagle and The Howling Wolf

Es superior, verdadero y hermoso,
Elevándose más alla de las nubes.
Aun cuando desciende a lo profundo de los valles,
Pone sus huevos el la cumbre más alta de las montañas.
Al otro lado esta el lobo con su rugido
Y ese lobo furioso y aullante se identifica
Con lo peor que está dentro de mi.
Él devora mis caídas y se justifica
Con su presencia en la jauría.

¿Quien ganará esta gran batalla?
¡Aquel a quien yo alimente!

Few are the moments in time when we, and everything around us seems extraordinary and unique; more often we feel like a tiny speck in the vastness of the universe.

The past is memory,
The present is passion,
And the future is desire.

We should always remember where we came from, do everything with enthusiasm, and have a vision for the future.

Adjusting to Family Life Without the Children

The eagle flies! When our children left the nest, our lifestyle slowed down. They had graduated from international management and financial business schools and contributed their experiences to my business ventures.

Claudia María and Lucía Carolina adapted completely to American culture while respecting and honoring their Hispanic traditions. They are a living symbol of the determination to succeed and to excel.

My husband has become my best friend and supports all of my endeavors. Together we are working towards a brighter future and a better world.

The vulnerability of baring my soul, the complexity of the English and Spanish languages, my health issues, family events, and community involvement were challenges I faced while writing this book. Nevertheless, the opportunity to share a life full of vicissitudes and self-discovery in the act of writing has given me the balance I seek in life.

All of the significant experiences and journeys with which I have been blessed are God's gifts and confirm that everything is possible. Being devoted and truthful to your mission and purpose in life will help you achieve your goals.

As we all travel along our path, we must maintain our personal beliefs, values, and principles. Most importantly, we must never forget our roots. At the same time, we must embrace other cultures. Yes, we will encounter challenges and be called upon to make sacrifices; nevertheless, we will have the satisfaction of knowing that our actions have helped to build unity and peace in the world.

By baring our souls and bringing business ethics, faith, and emotions together, we can achieve the balance so much needed in today's world. Even though we come from different cultural backgrounds and have varying personalities, we can realize what seems unattainable if we combine our hearts and souls with our actions, exercise rational behavior and act with integrity.

My philosophy applies to all things I do on behalf of others. I live each moment and pray to the Almighty for guidance so that I may see the results of my efforts with clarity. I strive for compassion, humility, and tolerance and hope they resonate with every one of my actions.

Being part of today's world gives me the perspective to

provide leadership and guidance with integrity and vision on a broad scale. This allows me to improve the lives of children and to educate them about their responsibilities as world citizens.

My life and the lives of those with whom I interact provide me with lots of surprises and wonderful opportunities to be a positive influence. I have discovered that material possessions are not a measure of power or influence; it is the footprint you leave on society that determines your influence.

To those I have encountered along my path who have encouraged me with their guidance, I will be forever grateful. I believe I have become more tolerant, less judgmental, and free of prejudices, and have a better understanding of the commonalities that exist among all people throughout the world.

I thank God each and every day for restoring my health and healing my wounds. The balance among my family, community, and my spiritual life gives me the peace I have always searched for; and the balance I have achieved among my body, mind, and spirit has restored my physical strength.

An Invitation:

In closing, I invite you to share my dream, to open yourself to the rest of the world and to build bridges of Unity and Peace.

I feel blessed in doing what I do: I build dreams... I build hope... I build opportunities.

My mission is to forge universal humanity into a unified tapestry of cultures; I challenge you to discover yours.

What is your mission?

Mongolia, The Land of my Ancestors and the Bridge Between East and West

With world brotherhood and peace through poetry,
We can unite nations in an effort to achieve
World peace and understanding.

People, places, time and space are priceless gifts the universe bestows upon us. Shortly after I had finished the first draft of this book, I was invited to join the World Academy of Arts and Culture and therefore encouraged by some authors to submit my book and to attend the XXVI World Congress in Ulaanbaatar, Mongolia, September 2006.

The mission of the World Academy of Arts and Culture, Inc. is to organize and celebrate a World Congress of Poets in different parts of the globe. The goals are to substitute peace for war in the minds of men, to promote world unity, and to engender the interchange of culture for mutual understanding of peoples from diverse cultures all of whom are striving for excellence in uplifting humankind.

The commemoration of the 800th anniversary of the Great Mongolian State was to take place. Mongolia has been a bridge between east and west since the earliest times and the opportunity to study the history and culture of all humankind was one I could not resist.

Dr. G. Mend-Ooyo, a distinguished Mongolian poet, President of the Mongolian Culture Foundation and Mongolian Academy of Culture and Poetry and President of the XXVI World Congress of Poetry selected my book as one that would celebrate this historical event.

"The translation of your book into Mongolian will truly be a gift that will help to connect the people of Mongolia, to the rest of the world," Dr. Mend-Ooyo later wrote to me.

I was honored by his request and responded:

"It is vital to me that I touch the heart of the Mongolian people with a message of unity and peace. They will see that across the mountains, steppes and oceans, live people just like them. We are all human beings united in our fervent desire to find peace and unity in our families, our communities, our governments, and most of all, in our hearts as we bear witness to the transformation of our world."

"Building Bridges of Understanding" offers a message of love and compassion and most of all, hope. This message was widely embraced at the congress of the more than 350 poets and artists who came from all over the world.

During the festivities, I presented my book to the country's president Nambariin Enkhbayar with a message from my native land Colombia and my adopted country, the United States of America. "I come to the land of my ancestors from the Americas and I have come to bond with the heart of the Mongolian people."

Lucía with Mongolian President Nambariin Enkhbayar
Surrounded by distinguished international authors

Gracias, Muchas Gracias

"Por favor" and *"gracias, muchas gracias"* were the words my mother encouraged us to learn in every language. To those whose paths have interconnected with mine on the journeys across the hemispheres, and most especially to my cherished friends whose souls have intertwined with mine down through the years, I send my heartfelt gratitude.

Gracias to you, Diane Diehl, my dearest and most loyal friend - *gracias* for the sustained purity of your vision throughout the years, which encouraged me to write this memoir. To Dr. MaryAnn MacEachern, CFRE, who is the most loyal enthusiast of my story. She used her anthropological and historic research in fact checking. To Roberto José Aragón, a man of great intellect and culture, a trusted friend, mentor and advisor whose poetic sense has often enriched my words.

To those involved with this project in the early stages I am deeply indebted. To John Carr, the graphic artist, for his digital wizardry in the preparation of the book's postcard and book cover.

To my husband Álvaro for his limitless patience, his constant dedication, loyalty, and unrequited love unending support throughout the many long days and countless sleepless nights I spent writing this book. I gratefully say, *Un millón de gracias, mi Amor.* To my daughters Lucía Carolina and Claudia María, my deep appreciation for their time selflessly spent reminiscing with me on the many family stories and anecdotes that appear in this book.

To my family in Colombia, especially my Giraldo brothers and sisters I send my everlasting love for the wonderful memories of experiences we shared together as children. They are: Marta Lía, Olga Cecilia, Henry, Oscar Humberto, Luz Stella, Iván Darío, whose support across the miles continues to inspire me, my sincerest appreciation for his contribution with the English-Spanish translations. To Luis Fernando, a kind and warm soul, a loving embrace for his continual reminders to look at life through a prism similar to the one I gave him on his second birthday, so that I may always see the true and wonderful colors of this world. And to the memory of my siblings Ligia Odila, Juan Adriano and Sergio Alfredo, and my sister-in-law Nancy García, guardian angels who with my mother are watching us from heaven.

Special thanks to Dr. Jane Goodall for illuminating my path to humankind, Mary Lewis for being the stairs to heaven, and all my friends and associates at the Jane Goodall Institute (JGI) worldwide who make all the difference in the world.

My sincere recognition to all the institutions and individuals with which I have collaborated over the years for supporting my goals. To the board members and trustees of National University, Western State University College of Law, the American Red Cross, the Society for the Advancement of Management, (SAM), Asociación Americana de Mexicanos en el Exterior (AAME), and the Latin Business Association (LBA).

To my mentor in the international business, Dan Young, for his invaluable and long-lasting friendship; he keeps me posted across the miles on global issues. To Jonathan Hutson who facilitated a series of innovative inter-group dialogues organized by the Multicultural Institute for Leadership (MIL) that brought together leaders from business, education, government, media, public interest groups, and faith communities.

And finally, to my readers who wish to learn about the roads I have traveled, the wisdom I have learned and the secrets I have discovered along the way, to where I am today… the answers are to be found within the pages of this book.

We all became part of the *Divine Plan.*

Bridge Builders of the 21st Century

Nuestros caminos se cruzaron,
nuestras almas se entrelazaron...

Our paths have interwoven,
our souls have merged...

It is extraordinary, that all through centuries, throughout times, throughout space, so many universes, throughout millions of people... we coincide–to paraphrase the Mexicanto *"Y coincidir."*

Gracias to those "bridge builders" it has been a blessing to know. They have been my friends, my role models, and every one of them in his or her own way has supported, encouraged, and inspired my mission. They are:

- Ambassador Ananda Guruge, from Sri Lanka, a supreme authority on the world's major religions, and an advisor on cultures, peace and unity.
- Antonio Ramon Villaraigosa, Mexican-American, first Latino Mayor of Los Angeles since 1872, considered one of the leading progressive voices in the country.
- Astronaut Buzz Aldrin, American, an adventurer in outer space, and his wife Lois.
- Dr. Amer El-Araf, Egyptian, president of the American European University Consortium, an environmental health specialist.

- Carlos Fuentes, Citizen of the world, one of Latin America's most prominent men of letters.

- Carlos Monsivais, Mexican author and environmentalist.

- Caribé, Argentinean-Brazilian modern art artist.

Christopher Cox, Chairman of the Securities and Exchange Commission (SEC) has made vigorous enforcement of the securities laws the agency's top priority.

- Daniel Villanueva, a pioneer and trailblazer, philanthropist with the Latino community in his heart.

- David Lizarraga, Mexican-American activist, a dynamic and visionary leader on education.

- Edward James Olmos, Mexican-American Actor and social activist.

- George Pla, President of one of the top civil engineering firms in the nation. He remains dedicated to civic leadership in the surrounding community in this Millennium.

- Honorable Elaine Chao, U.S. Secretary of Labor, for her mission of inspiring and protecting the hardworking people of America.

- Dr. Francisco J. Ayala, Spanish-American biologist and philosopher. Awarded 2001 National Medal Of Science.

- Harry P. Pachon, expert on immigration, Hispanic education issues, right issues, demographics and population analysis, and polling methodology.

- Hector Barreto Sr., Mexican, founder of the U.S. Hispanic Chamber of Commerce. He distinguished himself as a passionate advocate for small Hispanic businesses.

- Dr. Jerry C. Lee Chancellor, National University System a visionary for quality education.

- José Niño, international entrepreneur and business advocate.

- Jesus Chavarria, Publisher of the Hispanic Business Magazine, is the bridge between corporate America and Latino business.

- Juan Lladro, Spaniard, one of the founders of the Lladro porcelains.

- Kirov Ballet from Leningrad, the legendary Mariinsky Theater.

- Moctezuma Esparza, multitalented award-winning filmmaker, producer, entertainment executive and entrepreneur.

- Nely Galan, Cuban, a trailblazer, producer of English and Spanish language television programming for audiences in the United States and Latin America.

- Rueben Martinez, Mexican-American, winner of the prestigious MacArthur Fellowship award for his work to promote literacy in the Latino community.

- Rudy Beserra, Mexican-American, role model for Latinos who have made outstanding achievements in the corporate business world as an ambassador for the community.

- Sting, his wife Trudy and Sir Elton John, for their work with the Rain Forest Foundation.

- Tony Robbins, recognized authority on peak performance.

- Vicente Fox Quezada, President of Mexico, and his wife Marta Sahagun. Fox's term has been marked by an unprecedented economic stability and by a democratic atmosphere that is new to Mexico.

Webster Guillory, Orange County Assessor, a man of achievement with extensive experience in private and public sector

- William T. Esrey, Former Chairman and Chief Executive Officer of Sprint Corp widely recognized for developing, engineering and deploying state of the art network technologies.

- William Habermehl, honored by the United States Office of Education for his work as Orange County Superintendent of Schools. He oversees more than 530,000 students.

My Favorite Ones

When asked to name the people, the stories, the places, the books and the movies that I consider my favorites, I always think about those that have had the most influence on me to be the person I have become. Perhaps this exercise will help you to identify those that have helped to make you who you are today.

These are my favorites.

Children's Stories

- Aladdin
- Cinderella
- Little Red Ridding Hood
- The Ugly Ducking

What are your favorite ones? Why? ________________

____

____

____

____

People in History:

- The founders of all the great religions: Buddha, Jesus Christ, Muhammad.
- Confucius
- Leonardo da Vinci
- Abraham Lincoln
- Símon Bolívar
- Mohandas Gandhi

What are your favorite ones? Why? ______________

____

____

____

____

Classical Music

- Claire de Lune, Claude Debussy
- Concierto de Aranjuez, Joaquin Rodrigo
- The Four Seasons, Antonio Vivaldi
- Nights in the Gardens of Spain, Manuel de Falla.

What are your favorite ones? Why? ______________

____

____

____

____

Sacred Places I Have Visited

- Angkor Wat, Cambodia
- Ancient Cities & Gobi Sands in Mongolia
- Kyoto Temples, Japan
- Le Père Lachaise Cémenter, Paris, France
- Museum of Qin Terracotta Warriors, Xi'an, China
- The mysterious Salvador, Bahia, Brazil
- San Sebastián de Garabandal, Santander, Spain
- Teotihuacán, Mexico
- The Walled City of Cartagena, Colombia

What are your favorite ones? Why? ______________

____

____

____

____

Animals

- The Dove
- The Duck
- The Swan
- The Seagull
- The Eagle

What are your favorite ones? Why? ________________

____

____

____

____

Books

- The Bible
- Care of the Soul, by Thomas Moore
- Conversations with God I, II and III, by Neale Donald Walsch
- Illusions, by Richard Bach
- Le Petit Prince, by Antoine de Saint-Exupéry
- The Seat of the Soul, by Gary Zukav

What are your favorite ones? Why? ________________

____

____

____

____

Movies

- The Messenger, The Life of Joan d-Arc
- The Piano
- Il Postino
- Meet Joe Black
- Zorba the Greek

What are your favorite ones? Why? ________________

____

____

____

____

Artists and their Works of Art:

- Alessandro Botticelli, Primavera (The Birth of Spring, The Birth of Venus, and The Adoration of the Magi)
- Claude Monet (Waterlilies)
- Edgar Degas (Dancer on Stage)
- Georges Seurat (A Sunday Afternoon on the Island of La Grande Jatte)
- Paul Cezanne (Chrysanthemums)
- Paul Gauguin (Chemin a'Papeete)
- Pierre-Auguste Renoir (Luncheon of the Boating Party)
- Vincent Van Gogh (The Café Terrace on the Place du Forum, and Starry Night over the Rhone)

What are your favorite ones? Why? ________________

____

____

____

____

Gifts:

- From my grandfather, a telescope he used in the War of the Thousand Days, Panama
- From my grandmother, a wooden crucifix
- From my father, the book "La Historia de la Opera"

What are your favorite ones? Why? ________________

____

____

____

____

Favorite Authors and their Books

- Carlos Castañeda (Viaje a Ixtlan)
- Gabriel García Márquez (Cien Años de Soledad)
- Miguel de Cervantes Saavedra (Don Quijote)
- The works of William Shakespeare

What are your favorite ones? Why? ____________

____

____

____

____

Statements of Unity and Peace

What does Peace and Unity mean to you?

I asked this question to some of my friends from different walks of life I chose at random, and these were their unedited answers.

"Peace is more than the absence of war. It is tranquility within and without. It is the ability to live with self and with others. It means the ability to accept others with their differences and not demanding that they change. This is what unity is all about. Unless we can accept our differences, there will be no unity. Unity and oneness are not the same. Unity is the bridge that leads to oneness. True ecumenism has this for its foundation, the ability to live with differences and yet strive for unity. For a believer, there is always that sense of striving to fulfill this desire for unity, knowing it is willed by God." PAX.

– Fr. Anthony Delisi, O.C.S.O. Cistercian Monk

"Peace and unity begins with ourselves and is reflected in every relationship we have in the world–it starts with acceptance, love, understanding and compassion in all that we experience."

– Audis Husar, Colombian, Art Gallery Owner

"Peace for me means first of all to find your inner peace. Who hasn't made peace with each piece of their identity, will not be able to project peace outside. This inner peace is similar to feeling unity with others because once you reach acceptance for yourself; you accept others and become empathetic."

– Claudia Zysk, German, Intercultural Expert.

"Some people think that we are asking for some kind of utopia or perfection in mankind when we speak of Peace and Unity. However, a utopia or perfect situation is not necessary to have peace and unity in the world. What is necessary is the willingness of every peace-loving person to seek out commonalities in spite of differences and to solve problems with consultation rather than violence. These things are feasible and totally achievable one heart at a time." From my heart to yours,

– Emma Salahuddin, American, Educator

"Peace, in one form or another has been humanity's goal since the dawn of time, yet it continues to elude us. Unity, likewise, has rarely been achieved, but in no way has this deterred us from pursuing a seemingly unattainable objective.

Peace can be defined as a lack of conflict, while unity refers not only to a lack of conflict but to a mutual understanding and respect. These remain unattainable at the absolute level; relative progress, however, is perfectly possible. While the most visible agents of change work at an international level, progress at the individual level is fundamental, for while peace might be achieved through diplomacy the mutual understanding and respect necessary for unity must be embedded in members of society.

Peace may be a prelude to unity; once the former has been achieved, however, the latter becomes crucial to its maintenance, for without unity peace cannot and will not last."

– Dr. Marcus Holmlund,
Dutch-Colombian, Community Leader

"Peace and Unity are the perfect manifestation of the truth that lies deep within us when we are able to overcome the illusion of separation and realize that at the core of our being we are all One."

– Jesus Nebot, Spaniard Cinematographer

"Peace and unity allow us to see each other, as we truly are – brothers and sisters. Peace and unity are contagious gifts when we chose to be instruments of their service. A smile, a handshake or a kind word will plant the seeds of peace and unity into the hearts of any people. . . .anywhere, anytime, anyhow.

Peace and unity are the visible signs or fruits of love.

I believe that we are all called to be ambassadors of peace and unity.

Thank you Lucía for planting the seeds of peace and unity into the hearts of so many, including mine. You are a true ambassador of peace and unity."

– Tom Linnert, American, Community Builder

"Peace and Unity are more than words, they are actions. Actions which represent neighborly love and community well being. It is people caring about the less fortunate and blessing those more fortunate. It is treating others as you would treat your own family. It is living with a standard of self-respect and helping others maintain the same. It is an appreciation for diversity and allows the ability of all men to experience life without prejudice or fear. It is peace and unit."

– Víctor Elizalde, Mexican-American,
Corporate Leader

The Delaney Lucía and Brayden Álvaro Buehler García Trust was created on my grandchildren's name to assist the JGI program Roots & Shoots, which has groups in 96 countries. This program inspires youth of all ages to make a difference by becoming involved in their community to promote care and concern for animals, the environment, and the human community.

Index of Quoted Authors

Arias Sánchez, Oscar 123
Browning, Robert 104
Camus, Albert 88
Dalai Lama, The 156
Delisi, Anthony 199
De García, Lucía 75
Dinesen, Isak 152
Einstein, Albert 164
Elizalde, Víctor 201
Frost, Robert 63
Gibran, Kahlil 56
Goodall, Jane 15, 147
Guruge, Ananda 7
Hernández, Rafael 48
Holmlund, Marcus 200
Husar, Audis 199
Hutson, Jonathan 7
Jones-Ryan, Maureen 8
Juarez, Benito 115
King, Martin Luther 53
Kipling, Rudyard 169
Lincoln, Abraham 31
Linnert, Tom 201
Machado, Antonio 93
Mandela, Nelson 153
McCullough, Colleen 136
Mejia, Epifanio 32
Miller, Henry 21
Nebot, Jesus 200
Nitzche, Fredrick 37
Pope John Paul II 159
Robbins, Tony 8
Salahuddin, Emma 200
Serrano, Luis Martínez 49
Souviron, José Mariá 87
Standing Chief, Irving 44
Varela, Jairo 98
von Goethe, Johann Wolfgang 107
Young, Dan 7
Zysk, Claudia 199

About the Cover

There are no coincides! When I met Luis Sánchez, the Cuban- Mexican-Lebanese artist, a renaissance man who designed the book cover, it was a mutual cultural, spiritual and energy connection. We both knew it was the beginning of a long friendship. In our first conversation, I told him about the book I was writing and the art and vision of what the content was and so on. We then met several times wanting to know more about each other, about our desires, our ideals, and our passion for life. Luis wanted to spend more time with me to learn the essence of who I am.

We both discovered a unique respect for people and the universe. We agreed to go forth and working together. It became clear to Luis the responsibility he had to create something that represented a visual backdrop of what the book's message is about and traveled deep into his soul.

Luis began sketching ideas based on our meetings. When he surprised me with the preliminary drawing, I was captivated by his ability to grasp the spirit of my story: My fascination with the moon and the stars, my ancestry dating back to 1492, and the work I have done in the community across the globe becoming "a citizen of the world." I shared with Luis stories from childhood to my youth in Colombia helping the less privileged build their homes brick-by-brick. Thus, the idea of the da Vinci Bridge became a metaphor of building bridges for Unity and Peace. I am forever grateful to Luis for creating the book cover that speaks for itself. For fellowship and the love he demonstrated to my family and me.

Gracias Luis!

You may acquire the book *Building Bridges of Understanding, My Personal Quest for Unity and Peace* at a discount for business, educational, political and community Institutions, their employees and clients, friends and relatives.

TO PLACE AN ORDER USE THIS FORM

You can order by Phone: (949) 559-5507 or **E-mail:** Lucía.DeGarcía@cox.net
By Mail at Élan International 620 Newport Center Drive, Eleventh Floor
Newport Beach, California 92660 U.S.A.
For more information visit WWW.ELANINTL-USA.COM

Special price per unit US $21.95

For more than 10 books at US $18 each

Number of books to be purchased? ___________

Unit price $21.95 .... $__________

Unit price $18.00 .... $__________

California residents add 7.75% tax .... $__________

S & H add $3.95 for the first book and $2 for each additional book............ $__________

Total:.. $__________

Enclosed is my check payable to Elan International

Please charge my credit card # ______________________________

Visa Master Card Exp. Date (00/00)

Your Name: ______________________________

Company: ______________________________

Department: ______________________________

Address: ______________________________

____

Phone: ______________________________

E-mail Address: ______________________________

A portion of all proceeds to be donated to the Jane Goodall Institute (JGI)